The Wounded Chalice

Celebrating the Divinity of the Womb

by
Mary Grace

AuthorHouse™
1663 Liberty Drive, Suite 200
Bloomington, IN 47403
www.authorhouse.com
Phone: 1-800-839-8640

© 2008 Mary Grace. All rights reserved.

No part of this book may be reproduced, stored in a retrieval system, or transmitted by any means without the written permission of the author.

First published by AuthorHouse   3/26/2008

ISBN: 978-1-4343-6753-2 (sc)

Library of Congress Control Number: 2008901123

Disclaimer
The author, editors and publishers shall have neither liability nor responsibility to any person or entity with respect to any perceived loss or damages caused, directly or indirectly, by the information contained in this book. The events of this book are true but all of the names have been changed to protect the privacy of the individuals involved.

All rights reserved. No part of this book may be reproduced by any mechanical, photographic, or electronic process, or in the form of a phonographic recording; nor may it be stored in a retrieval system, transmitted, or otherwise be copied for public or private use---other than for "fair use" as brief quotations embodied in critical articles and reviews---without prior written permission of the author.

Cover design: ©2008 by Mary Grace

Printed in the United States of America
Bloomington, Indiana

This book is printed on acid-free paper.

I found *The Wounded Chalice* to be very special and unique and yet I could absolutely relate to some of your experiences as I have been there myself. Aspects of your experience and your approach were so novel and eye-opening for me. I could really feel your softness - the femininity and mother's love radiating through you and the strength and courage honed from your experiences.

I do so very much appreciate your bringing forth the message of sanctity and respect for our bodies and especially the feminine parts of our divine bodies. Thank you for your courageous heart, I shan't forget you.

Francie Gannon, M.A. Whole Systems Design

The Wounded Chalice is a candid and intimate look into one woman's journey toward self-acceptance and a heart felt reverence for her body. A story she lovingly shares so that others may also know the gifts of life so often taken for granted.

Ellan Catacchio, R.Y.T. Reiki Master

Table of Contents

PREFACE..ix

ACKNOWLEDGEMENTS..xiii

MESSAGE TO ME FROM MOTHER MARY........................xv

A MESSAGE TO THE READER FROM MOTHER MARY...........xvii

1   CHILDHOOD MEMORIES... 1

2   EXPERIENCES WITH THE FIRST MALES IN MY LIFE 13

3   TEEN YEARS INTO MARRIAGE 25

4   JOURNEY INTO MOTHERHOOD 35

5   YOUNG MOM OF TWO... 41

6   MIRACLE CHILD... 53

7   HONORING THE WOMB THAT BIRTHED ME 59

8   BETRAYAL OF MY CHILD 75

9   SINGLE PARENTHOOD 85

10   MY CHILDREN AS FORERUNNERS................................ 101

11   TRUSTING IN LOVE AGAIN - A DIFFERENT BETRAYAL........... 109

12	WISDOM COMES AT A HIGH PRICE	129
13	COLLEGE	139
14	BURIAL OF THE WOUNDED CHALICE	145
15	CALL OF THE DIVINE FEMININE	157

EPILOGUE 165

SURPRISE GIFT WAITING FOR YOU 168

A READER'S GUIDE 169

ABOUT THE AUTHOR 171

PREFACE

Fifteen years ago I was guided by the Divine Feminine to write about my experiences. God is both male and female; thus God is both Divine Masculine and Divine Feminine. This balance of the Divine can also be called Father/Mother God. It pleased me to be chosen for this task even though, at the same time, I was terrified at the thought of actually doing it. I know nothing about writing a book *per se*, so this is a conversation with all of you from my heart. Three separate times I started to put it down on paper but each time I set it aside.

This is the memoir of the many challenges I had in life, yet each challenge led me to understanding what unconditional love actually is. Motherhood is the prime example of that type of love. In becoming a mother, you are not a mother just until your child reaches maturity; you are a mother until the day you die. No love is stronger than maternal love and there is nothing more fierce than a mother protecting her child.

Our bodies are holy temples that contain the organs for perpetuating the human race. Imagine the awesome responsibility of being aware that without the womb, there would be no future generation. I did not honor that fact until I was faced with the prospect of losing that precious organ. I honored that part of me the only way I knew how; I demanded it back after its removal from my body.

For as long as I can remember, I had a burning desire to have children. I could not wait to become a mother as I saw this to be the fulfillment of my destiny. Motherhood totally fulfilled my yearning to *BE* love and *GIVE* love.

Until I was faced with the reality of needing a hysterectomy, I never contemplated the uniqueness of the womb. I never even wondered if I would be able to bear children. I simply took for granted that my ability to have children was there, waiting for the appropriate time when I would be able to fulfill my destiny. Had I not experienced being a mother I would never have fully appreciated the gift of having a womb and the miracles that would come forth.

The womb is the cradle of humanity, where new beginnings are given the opportunity to grow so that the whole world may partake. Within the womb lay the mystery and the beauty of creation. And not just in the children that come forth, for the womb is a microcosm of *All* Creation. Even though today we have ultrasound machines which can monitor the progress of the fetus, there is truly no way to measure the unfolding evolvement of a human life.

When it became evident that I needed a hysterectomy, my spirit just cringed at the thought of my womb being treated as just something that was surgically removed from my human body. This tiny organ allowed me to fulfill what I felt was my mission on earth; to be a mother. I could not allow it to be treated indifferently.

In order to explain how this book evolved, I will start with my own beginning which is the story of my childhood. I took motherhood for granted even as a child. It felt 'right" to assume that I would be a mother yet I never realized the twists and turns it would take to actually get me to the point of claiming and celebrating the divinity of the womb.

I went through all the phases of growing up to reach adulthood yet still did not fully recognize what unconditional love actually is. Motherhood taught me that. I had many opportunities to practice that particular kind of love. Today I know in my soul that *LOVE* encompasses and forgives all transgressions.

My hope is that my life experiences may bring remembrances that you are able to relate to and identify with. Perhaps they may bring some recognition of your own faith, love, and courage despite life's outward appearances.

Now, the Divine Feminine is asking me to complete this book that other women might honor their bodies, and in doing so, show the men how to honor theirs. We humans are gifted with a wonderful vessel for our Spirit which enables us to be here on earth, expressing who we are in such marvelous ways. We take our vessels for granted, but when we awaken to the gift of our bodies from God, we awaken to our joy. Joy comes when we are grateful for what we have and there is no joy greater than being one with our bodies and with Spirit.

There is so much for us to experience including the freedom to move about this planet with complete awareness of what it feels like to touch and be touched; to taste, to hear, to feel, to immerse ourselves in communion with all the forms of life that exist here. What a gift we can give to other souls through the miracle of perpetuating the human race. To the female readers of this book, I say:

THOU ART MY SISTER

Thou art my sister, because we were born of the same great spirit; conceived from the same mound of earth; slept quietly together in the cradle of unknowing until He in his gentleness set us in the midst of humanity… you are my sister, I love you.

You and I are destined to be companions on the highway of life; together or apart, you are my sister, I love you . . . if the color of my skin is different from yours, it mattereth not, only let the beauty of our souls be kindred . . .

I will honor your wisdom and understanding, as you will mine, together we shall seek the seeds of truth in the distant rooms of the Great Spirit; the reflection of inner knowledge shall wear as beauty upon our faces . . . you are my sister, I love you.

I will be human and fall down in rough places, but thy hand is near mine, I will reach for it, I shall not be alone. I will embrace you when the rains of sorrow visit you, I will befriend your soul as it were my own . . . you are my sister, I love you.

If death takes from me the lamp of life, and the veil of eternal sleep falls across my eyes before yours, I will wait for you, I will come to lead you across the bridge of night into the meadows of the Great Spirit . . .you are my sister, I love you.

Jean Humphrey Chaille

ACKNOWLEDGEMENTS

I am grateful for the urging and guidance of The Divine Feminine, without Her this book would not have come into existence.

I am grateful to my children for giving me the opportunities to experience the joys and challenges of being their mother.

I am grateful to Rose, my beloved friend since childhood, for the long walk she took to retrieve my precious womb.

I am grateful to Rhea, another dear friend who consoled me when my heart was torn apart as only a mother's could be.

I am grateful to Peggy Day, co-author of *Edgar Cayce on the Indigo Children*, who lovingly polished this book into a diamond with her skillful editing.

I am grateful to Patricia (Trisha) Zierler, R.M.T., K.H.M., author of the CD – *Embrace Your Sacred*, who lovingly and truthfully exposed my redundant rambling.

I am grateful to Christine Krupa Fiel, M.A., C.N.H.P., author of *How to Love Yourself*, whose editing and mastery of words allowed my story to unfold with clarity and continuity.

I am grateful to Scott W. Gonnello, author of *Climbing the Food Chain*, for his graphic printing enabling the cover of this book to stand on its own in all its glory.

I am grateful to Edward T. Mish, silversmith and inventor of *Mish's Silver Polish* which is used in museums around the world, whose patience and expertise repaired my beloved Chalice.

I believe that we are all human angels mysteriously placed in each other's paths to convey a message or to give us an opportunity to transform this earthly life into a reflection of the Divine Love that Mother/Father God showered upon us. For this, I am grateful.

I am grateful for the privilege of sharing part of my life's story with you, the reader. My sincere wish is that it may help you acknowledge the *COURAGE* and *LOVE* within yourself. Your body serves you on this planet; it is a temple of your Spirit. Bless and honor the physicality which allows you to give another soul the opportunity to live on this beloved sphere called Earth.

MESSAGE TO ME FROM MOTHER MARY

Yes, my child, I am speaking to you about your book, the book that will bring the *Love* of the Divine Feminine to this planet Earth. You are a creation of the divine, excitingly birthed into this biosphere to experience. As a creation, you bring into being your own experiences in order to know yourself more fully. Know that all experiences are Divine, even as it does not feel divine.

You dreamed of knowing both sides of any experience so that you may fully appreciate the opposite. If you were never cold, you would never appreciate being warm. If you were never hungry, you would never be satiated. If you were never unhappy, you would never know happiness. To appreciate success, one must understand the struggles of the unsuccessful.

This will be a book about your hysterectomy. You obeyed the word as it was given to you, you played your part well and the culmination was perfect. It is time for the world to hear your message. It is time for all to know about honoring their body and their body's wisdom.

You were destined to be the first to honor your body in such a way. You revere life in all its forms and you are grateful for the opportunity to birth and nurture the lives you brought forth. Although your children do not understand nor appreciate what you have done, nevertheless, they love you as their mother.

Know that I am with you at each moment, even to the end of time as you know it. Many miracles will happen; many hearts will be open. Allow your heart to be as pure as white snow and as open as a huge corridor opening into eternity. Love yourself as I love you. See yourself as I see you.

Mother Mary

A MESSAGE TO THE READER FROM MOTHER MARY

Beloved reader let me tell you a story about a woman who is pure, honest and forthright. She has put motherhood above all else and still continues to do so. Her Love for humanity and especially her own children knows no bounds. Let her Love speak to you at levels that you are ready to hear. She so loved being a mother that she could not allow her womb to be treated in any way other than with respect and love for what it enabled her to do: become a mother. She resisted the authority of the doctors and this, in itself, was unusual, as she had always esteemed the medical profession. As a child she was taught that others knew more than she did.

When it was decided, after many misgivings, that she was to have a hysterectomy, she refused—unless the doctors agreed to return her womb to her. Of course this shocked the doctors but they agreed to confer. After much discussion, they decided to allow it to be returned to her with the condition that a biopsy of the uterus be performed. Her uterus—her womb—the haven where her children whom she loved unconditionally were carried, was now not under their authority without conditions.

Life has taught her the value of being a woman and the delight of having a physical body to experience life on this beloved planet. She is an ordinary human being who came to Earth to remember the truly remarkable power of the human heart and the love that is everywhere and in everything. How could it be any other way, as Love comes from the Divine?

1
CHILDHOOD MEMORIES

I am a woman of seventy years of age. I have seen much, felt much, lived much, and am grateful for the opportunity to continue doing the same. Our beloved Mother Earth is a school that we have chosen to come to for experiences in a world of duality. In our procession along the paths of learning, we show our love by sharing what we have learned in the hopes that others will benefit. My experiences have been unique to me and I hope to share with you what I have garnered from each episode.

I grew up in a very dysfunctional home with a brutal father, naïve mother, and three brothers - one older and two younger. The oldest was quite a bully and I tried to protect my younger brothers with my equally dysfunctional attempts at mothering.

My father owned a small farm, where I was born, and we were quite poor. In those days, poverty was not such a stigma as most of the people we knew were in the same boat as us. As a child, you don't know anything different if there is no one to compare your life to. Even if there was, it is not until you get to perhaps the third grade that you are mature enough to be aware of any difference.

There was no transfer station, dump or trash pick up. In fact, there was a pile in the yard where we threw all the nondegradable junk; the garbage was reprocessed into mulch.

We had chickens and of course a rooster. One day, I was outside nibbling on a cracker. I was about a year and a half old so I was still a toddler. The rooster decided he wanted a bite of my cracker and as he was larger than me, I ran away from him crying: "Mommy, Mommy!" The faster I tried to run, the faster he ran after me.

Before my mom could reach me, I ran onto the pile of junk to get away from him. I fell down on a piece of glass, slicing my left hand deep enough to require stitches. When I was brought to the family doctor, he agreed that it needed stitches. I was terrified of the needle he would have to use to "freeze" the area before he could start stitching. I wonder if I had ever been pricked by a needle, thus knowing the pain it could cause.

I guess I created quite a stir, screaming all the while and not letting the doctor near me. My mother eventually promised me that he would not sew me up so I quieted down enough to let him near me. The doctor finally pulled the gap closed and used tape to keep it closed so the bleeding would stop.

My mother loved me so much and could not bear to hear me cry. It hurts the heart of every mother to hear her child scream. A mother's knee jerk reaction is to save her child no matter why the child is crying. Her love knew no bounds and she supported me through it all. I still have the scar to this day.

We lived at the farm until I was two years old. Then we moved about two hours away to another town and city. My family rented an apartment for two years which is where I remember the large barrel sitting under the gutter's drain pipe. The rain water from the drain ran into it, and was stored there until it was needed.

I remember it being used only to rinse my hair but I am sure it had other uses. It was Mother Nature's creme rinse and hair conditioner. It is very difficult to comb long hair without a lot of crying and this eased the tangles.

We only took showers or baths and washed our hair on Saturday so we would be fresh for church on Sunday. This was before there were any Masses said on Saturday night.

My mom used to set my hair with rags to make the pipe curls. Boy, were they difficult to sleep on.

We were living there when World War Two finally came to a halt. I did not understand why everyone was so happy. Car horns were honking, and flags were flying.

Because of the war rations, we could not get butter. We ate white lard with a small round drop of orange coloring to make it look like butter. It was a lot of fun to put that colored drop into the plastic sheathing that held the lard and then squeeze it until it all looked like real butter.

At long last we were able to buy a new home in the same town. It was a two story building with a chicken coop attached to a garage and a carport joining the garage to a barn in the backyard. We had a huge piece of land that we farmed in the summer, canning most of the crops for the upcoming winter season. Being the only girl, I was my mom's only helper in cutting and canning all the fruits and vegetables for the cold weather when fresh produce would not be available.

I remember the cherry tree in our yard that gave us wonderful succulent cherries. My mom made such delicious pies with them. We could hardly wait until they were red enough to pick. Two of my brothers fell out of the tree and broke their arms while picking them but it did not stop them from climbing it.

We had chickens again but I was big enough now so that I could not be intimidated by a rooster. In fact, one of my chores was collecting the eggs.

My dad would order the baby chicks and we had what looked like a huge upside down funnel where the light and the heat allowed them to grow. This heating instrument was in the upstairs bedroom so I got to play and handle them all I wanted. Of course, the opposite of that was getting upset when one of the chicks died which would inevitably happen.

In the winter we sold Christmas trees from Canada in our yard for extra money. That was the chore of my brothers. I was not big enough to handle the trees but I got to take the money and keep track of what we made. Perhaps this is where my love of numbers began.

There was a lot of tall grass that grasshoppers liked which made it easier for us children to catch them. We used to make a game of it to see who could catch the most but we would let them go afterwards.

When we played hide and seek, it was fun to climb onto the roof of the chicken coop, then onto the garage roof and then onto the carport roof where we were not very visible. I don't think my parents ever caught us climbing on the roofs or we would have been reprimanded.

My friend Rose and I used to love to play dress up. We would borrow clothes like scarves, hats, gloves, and shoes from our mothers. Then we would pretend we were all grown up while we clomped around in shoes too big for us. I know little girls still do that to this day.

Something that I no longer see is little girls making clothing from crepe paper. Rose and I would make all kinds of costumes from different colors. One thing about crepe paper was that it would stretch so we could wrap it around us and create all kinds of different costumes. If it rained, then it would really stretch and the dye would run all over us. What fun we had.

I also liked to pretend to be grown up by imitating the adults; what child doesn't! One day I took brown corn silk that was all dried up and rolled it in toilet paper like a cigarette and lit it. It tasted awful but I felt like I was doing what the adults did. I felt grownup. I never got caught doing that either. Where did I get my role models for cigarette smoking? The funny thing is, my mother did not smoke and my father only smoked a pipe.

It is amazing how the adults and peers in our lives have such an influence on us. As a child, you are not aware of this influence and I know I was not fully aware of my influence on others until I reached the age of 40.

Since we needed money, my father decided to remodel the barn in back of the house. We could live there while he rented out the front house. In the remodeling phase during the winter, he moved us down into the cellar of the front house where the only room that had a wall was the bathroom.

Besides the slab of concrete in the kitchen area, the bathroom was the only other part of the cellar that had concrete. There were only a toilet and shower in there.

The rest of the basement was all sand. Do you know what grows in sand? Fleas!!!! It was difficult sleeping because we were always being bitten. This was set in my mind as the first bedroom I would remember. I wish I could remember the bedroom before this one but diverse circumstances seem to implant in my memory deeper than ordinary ones.

There were two very deep sinks called set tubs on the only other slab of concrete and they were used for laundry. It was the only area that had running water. Our kitchen table and chairs were placed there.

The washing machine was also permanently placed there because it was on wheels and was not moveable in the sand. It was the old wringer type where you washed the batches of clothing according to color because the wash water was not changed between batches. We started off with hot water, soap and bleach. Then we washed the white clothing first, then the medium colored clothing and then the dark colored clothing. By the time we got to the dark batch, there was no more bleach power, the water was cool and it was quite dirty looking.

It did not matter if the water was dirty because you couldn't tell on the dark clothes anyway. To this day, I still wash according to color with the white batch being first. Habits from childhood are so ingrained that they carry into adulthood.

There were two deep set tubs so the washing machine was wheeled to the first one, the clothes put through the ringer into the clear water from the wash water and then the wringer was turned to face the other tub where the clothing went into the next tub of clean water.

I had to be very careful not to have the clothes bunch up as they went into the wringer because then it would jam or the clothes would wrap around the rollers. It was necessary to make sure the towels, clothes, etc., were flat so they would go through without jamming and to wring the most amount of water out so they would dry more quickly.

It was also very important not to let your fingers or sleeves get caught by the wringer or your whole arm would go through the mashing rollers. After getting my fingers mashed once, I learned to be very careful. It is such a scary feeling to watch as your hands and arms are going through the rollers and you are powerless to stop them. The rollers keep going until someone hits the release to open them up. I learned to hit the release as soon as I noticed some of the clothing being caught or my sleeves getting jammed under them.

If Monday were rainy, the wet clothes were hung on the clotheslines above our beds so they could dry as this was the only place in the cellar where this could be done. Taking a nap was not a good idea until the clothes were dry. Luckily, in those days we only washed on Mondays. Each day was dedicated to a specific chore. You probably guessed that Tuesday was ironing day.

Home made baked beans and hot dogs were the staple on Saturday night. Sundays we always had a meat roast of some kind. We all had three sets of clothing, one for school, one for play and one for Sunday best. As I look back to those days, I see there was so much order in our lives then. We even had a day each week to celebrate having nothing to do and just relaxing together. I am chuckling as I am writing this because now I realize that moms never get a day off.

The huge black wood stove had four things that looked like burners except they were solid and were always hot when the stove was in use. You could not turn them off or on; they just were hot if you were feeding wood to the stove for heat or cooking. Cooking in those days was quite an art. Can you imagine not having a temperature control on your burners or oven? On the side of the oven was the door to load the wood into the stove.

It was fun to put our feet on the edge of the oven to warm them during the winter. Our big black stove was great in that it dried clothes so nicely. Another feature was hanging your socks or mittens on a shelf above the stove; they felt so good when you put them on.

My activities were not spectacular. We children did not get allowances so we needed to earn our money in other ways. I would take care of a little girl on Sundays so that her parents could go to Church and I would get paid a quarter. Boy, did I feel rich. That quarter enabled me to go the movies for fourteen cents and have eleven cents to spend on popcorn, ice cream or candy.

I still remember walking about 3 miles with my best friend to the only theater within walking distance for the Sunday matinee.

We would walk down a hill and then take a short cut to the movie theatre by sliding down a steep dirt path right after a bridge that spanned the railroad tracks. We must have gotten quite dirty doing that, but I don't recall.

What a choice I had to make every week: popcorn or ice cream! It felt like a very difficult choice as I wanted them both. I had a penny left so then there was the choice of penny candy or bubble gum.

Looking back at all my memories, life was so simple then. We had ice deliveries because there was no such thing as a refrigerator. We had an ice box and it required ice to keep the food cold. It was much smaller than our refrigerators today.

When the ice man came, it was our delight to get a chip of ice from the block that he was chipping to make it small enough to fit in the top of the icebox. On a hot summer day, that chip of ice really hit the spot.

Groceries were bought on a daily basis from our neighborhood grocery store; there was no way to keep the food fresh in such a small space allotted by our icebox. If food were needed, we kids could go to the store and get what was needed and it was put on our bill which was paid later.

Milk delivery was an everyday occurrence in our neighborhood. It was not pasteurized or homogenized. It came in a quart bottle with the cream on the top. We would always skim off the cream for coffee or to make whipped cream or for whatever else we needed it for.

All the baking was done at home; there were no bakeries to buy from. We made our own doughnuts, cookies, cupcakes, breads and all manner of desserts.

In the summer, my best friend and her family went to a lake every Sunday. We kids would go swimming and the grownups would prepare the cookout. Her parents were kind enough to include me and they even furnished the food I ate.

Looking back, I realize now that my friend's family was aware of the abuse I was suffering at home and they took this opportunity to spirit me away for some fun times. My gratitude to them knows no bounds.

That was the life. It was the only day I could feel free of all the bullying and the abuse. Yet, ironically it was the place where I learned to swim and to also fear the water. There was a raft that everyone swam out to and just to reach it was incentive enough for me to learn how to swim.

One day, I had almost reached it when the older boys decided to tease me. They would not let me climb on the raft. They kept pushing me away from it until I was so tired that I actually started to drown. I knew I was drowning and I have no idea how I finally got up on the raft to rest.

After that, I always had a fear of my feet not touching the bottom when I was in the water. From that time on, I lost the joy and freedom of swimming as I stayed closer to shore to keep my feet solid on the ground.

It was so wonderful to have a best friend who lived right on my street. We could walk to and from school together. In the winter, since we had no snow removal at that time, the plows pushed all the snow to the edge of the road which formed huge mountains of snow against the shoveled sidewalks. We kids always enjoyed sliding down the ends of those snow mountains on our way to and from school. We would do that on our butts or if you were brave, you would stand up and slide down on your boot covered feet.

We enjoyed such simple pleasures as children. We played outside most of the time and there was a myriad of games we would play.

Do any of you remember taking a can and smashing it in the middle with your foot so it kind of wrapped itself around your shoe? We would use any cans we could find, soda or beer, it did not matter. Then we would clomp down the sidewalk or on a driveway keeping in cadence with our steps. We sounded like horses and we could go slow or gallop. Such fun we had.

I remember one time when my friend and I liked the same boy who lived on our street. She was mad at me about this situation, yet we remained friends the way only best friends can be, even after she had this boy wipe my face with snow as we cut through a snow covered field on our way to school. It is always amazing to me the events that occur in our lives over the opposite sex. It is a part of childhood and childish memories of my youth. I cherish all the memories of our friendship even the disagreements we had.

Now back to telling you about my childhood living quarters. We moved out to the barn and I finally had my own bedroom upstairs with a big closet to boot. The mice used to run under my bed at night but I was not frightened of them. After living down in the cellar, this seemed like paradise. Our heat was hot air fueled by coal and there was a grate in the downstairs floor and one at the head of the stairs upstairs. It was fun to stand on the grate and the warm air would heat my legs as it blew my skirt around.

Our floor in the living room was still the old barn boards with the wide spaces in between. In fact, the only rooms that had linoleum were the kitchen and bathroom. To keep the dust down as I swept it, I sprinkled the barn board floors with water. The sprinkler (a bottle with holes at the top) did double duty, sprinkling the clothes before we ironed and sprinkling the floors so they could be swept. Remember this was before wash-and-wear or permanent press material was discovered. Everything was made from cotton which required ironing.

I remember sprinkling the clothes, rolling them up and putting them in the icebox (before we graduated to a refrigerator) so that the dampness would be even throughout the material. It certainly made the ironing easier, but I still hated to iron.

At one point in my married life, we could only afford one modern washing appliance and I chose an electric clothes dryer over getting an automatic washing machine. I preferred using the old wringer type washing machine to having to hang the clothes outside in the winter, then bringing them into thaw and having to iron them. With today's clothing material, if your clothes are put in an electric dryer, they don't need ironing.

My younger brothers were supposed to help me with the dishes but they were good at hiding when it was time for them to dry the dishes that I had washed. Many the times I would have to climb out of my bedroom window onto the roof on the second floor. I would grab them off the roof where they had climbed to avoid doing the dishes.

The modern invention, the telephone, became available to the general public while we were living in the barn. That was such a new commodity. To actually be able to speak to someone anywhere in the world was quite a miracle indeed. Before that, a letter was the only way to communicate and it took so long to receive the latest news.

We had party lines on our phone which used one long ring, two short rings and a combination of short and long rings. Each family was assigned their own pattern of rings so we had to wait until the ringing stopped for a minute to be sure whose ring it was before we could pick it up. The phone company did have private lines but they were quite expensive.

We could eavesdrop on what people were saying if we kept our house quiet so they would not know we were listening. Five-way conversations were also quite possible and did happen. In fact, I still today listen for the dial tone before I dial the number I am calling. Old habits die hard for we were often scolded for making so much clicking noise when we dialed and there was someone already on the line.

There was no such thing as calling up your friend to play. We would go to each other's houses and call their names from outside until they would come out to play. I do not know why we did not knock on their doors but we always shouted their names until they came out or we were invited inside.

I was 11 years old when TVs were invented or should I say when I became aware of them. We could not afford one so we used to go to the hardware store and watch the programs on a big television set from outside through the store's window where they had placed it. We enjoyed all the radio programs though; each family at least had a radio.

The radio programs were: The Lone Ranger, Green Hornet, Hermit's Car, Let's Pretend and Grand Central Station and many more that I cannot remember. The whole family as a unit would sit around the radio and listen which was usually on Saturday night.

2
EXPERIENCES WITH THE FIRST MALES IN MY LIFE

When I was 5 years old, my new baby brother, William, was born. My only desire was to mother him with all the love I had to give. I had no idea how to care for his physical needs and I was not even aware of what those needs might be. I remember one day, I was rocking him in his carriage on the porch when the carriage rolled off the porch suddenly and landed upside down. I ran to my mother crying, "I killed my baby brother! I killed my baby brother!"

Mother came running and was quite upset as she saw the carriage. She lifted the carriage and, lo and behold, William was just lying there looking up at her. He wasn't even crying. She lifted him into her arms and also consoled me as I was the one sobbing.

I really enjoyed William. I was small in body stature and William was quite a chubby baby so it wasn't long before I had trouble carrying him around. In fact, I remember holding his body in front of mine and waddling while he just gurgled.

I was too young when I first started school as my father brought me to the nuns when I was only 4 years old and insisted that I start first grade. They were in fear of my dad so they allowed it. I was so scared of being left there alone and being in a place that was quite foreign to me, but I knew better than to disagree with my dad. There was no such thing as kindergarten back then, consequently I was always the youngest in the class.

When I came home from school that first afternoon, my mom grabbed me and was sobbing out loud. She knew I was too young to go to school. She had had no idea that this would happen so she had not prepared me either mentally or physically. Even if she had known, I can't imagine that she would have been allowed to do anything.

Mom must have been so disappointed! She had so looked forward to dressing me up especially for my very first day of school. As I was the only girl, she had been cheated of a very important day in my life and in hers.

My next brother Charlie was born when I was nine-and-a-half years old. By now I was bigger physically and mature enough to really enjoy an infant.

After practicing on William, I felt more confident of myself and I was more reliable. I took care of him quite often. In those days, girls of ten-to-twelve years of age were allowed to care for children.

I would bring Charlie to school with me sometimes when his sitter could not care for him. The nuns were allowed to be more lenient in their school and the law allowed a lot more interaction with families. He followed me everywhere. Most of the time, I didn't mind.

One of the difficulties in living down in the cellar was not having a place I could escape to. I always tried to avoid my oldest brother, Andy. He was really cruel to me and my two younger brothers.

Perhaps he learned his cruelty at the hands of our father.

I was terrified of spiders and did not know why. My mother eventually told me much later in life that when I was little he would shut me in the closet and tell me that the spiders were in there crawling all over me.

The cellar where we were living before we moved to the barn was infested with daddy long leg spiders. It was almost impossible to stay away from them because they were in the rafters that could hide them and the lighting was poor.

One day, I saw Andy and his pals coming into the cellar. I knew something was up. His pals surrounded me and then held my arms behind my back. I was so frightened.

"Let me go!" I shouted.

There was no one else home and although I screamed and hollered, no one heard me. I squirmed and kicked but all I succeeded doing is getting my arms hurt more as I struggled.

I can still see his smirking face and glinting eyes as he took a giant daddy long leg spider and one by one pulled off the legs and threw them on me.

"Please let me go," I pleaded.

"No, don't do that," I begged.

He was so happy to be causing me to cry out in terror. I don't think his friends enjoyed my dilemma as much as he did. He was facing me all the while. It felt like this went on for hours but I am sure it didn't.

Finally the body of the spider was the only part left and he laughed out loud as it landed on me. I screamed so loud and cried until I got the hiccups but it did no good; they just laughed at me. If I told on him, he would beat me up so I had to keep quiet about this torture.

Perhaps this is a good place to tell the story of how I conquered my fear of spiders and when it finally released its grip. My husband and I went on a picnic with friends when my oldest son was only one and a half years old. I was lying on the blanket with him so he would take a nap when suddenly I noticed a spider on his back.

With no forethought, only panic and reaction, I got up and started running away from him. He, of course, was frightened so he ran after me calling: "Mommy, Mommy!"

I finally stopped running. I was so mortified. How could I run away from my own son? I was supposed to protect my child from all dangers even if that included spiders.

After this episode, I made up my mind to conquer that fear so that my children would not inherit my fear of nature.

In those days, I had no clothes dryer. If the clothes were not dry when I had to bring them in from outside, I hung them up again on clotheslines in the back hallway. That was usually where I saw spiders. I wonder if it is moisture that draws them to certain places.

When I did spot them, I would freeze. Then I would gather all my courage to move and get my husband's shoes to kill it. I could not use my own shoes; just the thought of it brought shivers to my body.

I would shake all over after I killed them but I was determined to conquer my terror of spiders. After about 6 months to a year of doing this, I graduated to using my own shoes.

Boy was that difficult! Fear is not conquered in a minute; it takes consistent awareness of its power over you. Each time you make a decision to face that fear, it strengthens you and the fear lessens. Eventually you take your power back.

I loved my children so much that I would do even this for them. This was just the beginning of having the courage to surmount my challenges through love. Maternal love conquers all, even the greatest of fears.

Although my father was abusive, I have to thank him for my spirituality and love of Jesus. He was a very strict and devout Catholic. Every night we all knelt around our parents' bed and said the Rosary.

My desire to be a nun was always very strong even though I felt even more strongly that motherhood was my calling. At that age, I could not conceive of a way to be as close to Jesus as I perceived a nun to be. Yet I also wanted to be married and be a mother.

I had no conception of unwed mothers. I knew no one who was because we had no television so my world view was quite small. In my mind, mothers were always married.

I fell in love with Jesus and although Mother Mary and God were supposed to be important, in my small mind I saw only Jesus. I cannot explain my devotion to Him except to say that I felt His Love for me to the bottom of my soul. Thus began my love affair with Jesus.

At that time, the awareness of the Divine Feminine had not even surfaced. I must have felt the gentleness of God's feminine side because I could not feel Him as a vengeful God and still cannot today. Only humans are vengeful but God gave us free will as a gift and will not take back what He has given. He could stand right in front of you when you were preparing to do something terrible but He could not stop you unless you gave Him permission. We cannot control what someone else does to us but we can control our "reaction" to what has happened.

In those days, the Church rules were quite different from today. You did not eat meat on Friday and in order to receive Holy Communion it was mandated that you fast from midnight the night before.

My favorite time of the year was Lent as I would be allowed to attend Mass every morning and receive Holy Communion. The statues were covered in purple and it felt like we had more church ceremonies that used incense during that time. I loved to hear the clanking of the censer as it was swung in all directions, spreading that fragrance to every part of the church. My mom would make me a deviled egg sandwich and hot cocoa that I would eat afterward before school began.

An episode that has stuck in my mind was the day I was talking to a priest in a small convenience store across from the Church. I must have been asking him questions. I remember asking him about my little girl cousin because I had heard that only Catholics go to heaven and she was Protestant. I could not believe that story so I thought I would ask an expert.

He said that it was true, only Catholics can go to heaven. I remember getting so indignant. I placed my hands on my hips with my legs apart and said very loudly, "My God would not do that!"

Nothing he said would change my mind. My God was the Father who loved all people. To this day, I believe this in the deepest recesses of my soul. God the Father was kind and was good to all.

My brother Andy and I delivered the daily newspaper together. One day I guess I was slowing him down because I did not have a bike. He told me to get on his bike and he would give me a ride.

I decided to sit sidesaddle like a lady instead of straddling it like I would normally. It was in the winter, and I had boots and heavy socks on. He went over a bump and in went my right foot, right into the spokes.

I guess it surprised me so much that I was in shock; I don't remember feeling any pain. My brother brought me to the home of one of our customers, and upon seeing my predicament, they drove me home. My dad drove me to the doctor's office.

It was a good thing he was home as my mom did not have her driver's license and did not get one until she was in her forties. It seems the boot saved my foot because after they had cut the boot and sock away, my heel was hanging only by threads, in which gratefully were the nerves necessary for a full recovery.

The thickness of the boot and the heaviness of my sock took the first brunt of the circular spokes. My dad took me for an ice cream cone afterward. It was the only time I remember him buying me a treat, so it was a very special day to me.

We could not afford two crutches so I only had one. Andy was supposed to help me walk to school but as soon as he was out of Mom's eyesight, he took off as I tried to hobble my way on one good foot and one crutch.

I remember my sixth-grade teacher picking me up and carrying me up the stairs because our classroom was on the second floor. At that time, I thought she was tall and strong. She appeared to be. Yet, when I met her 20 years later, she was only 4'10" so she couldn't have been as tall as I had perceived when I was little.

Although my heel was stitched back to my foot and the stitches all around the heel were healing nicely, the skin kept growing out like a little growth in the area on the inside of my ankle. I would have to make weekly trips to have the knob cauterized so I would have smooth skin on my inner ankle later on.

I finally graduated to doing the paper route by myself. I did a great job if I do say so myself. One of my greatest lessons was learned not from delivering the newspaper but from the proceeds.

I was new to handling the money and I knew the man came to collect it every other week. Whatever was left after I paid him was what I had earned. Then one week, for some unknown reason, I was having cravings for ice cream and candy. I would "borrow" a few cents here and a few cents there from the container I placed the money in.

One day I realized that I may not have enough to pay for the newspapers. I was not sure how much I owed but it felt like I had taken a huge amount from the money I had collected.

I kept it down in the cellar on top of the furnace that heated the front house, the same cellar where we had lived before. I could easily take money without anyone seeing me.

When the collection day came, I made sure I was nowhere around so no one could find me to ask me where all the money was. I was hiding so no one would find me.

To this day, no one ever asked me about the money and I do not know who paid the newspaper man but….I learned not to spend any money again until I had earned it and it was in my hands. I had been terrified and felt like I had received a reprieve.

On one rare occurrence, my dad took my mom out for a treat. They were walking back home and my dad was carrying a box. Being just a child, I ran up to him.

"Is that for me daddy?" I cried.

He said: "Yes, it is."

He gave it to me and I ran all the way home. I was so excited; I couldn't wait to open it. When I opened it, it was a raincoat for my mom. I was crushed! My dad had lied to me. I was happy for my mom because she never got presents but I never believed my dad after that. Isn't it amazing the things that stick with you from your childhood?

As children we live always in the present time, there is no past and no future therefore the really hard parts of our childhood do not seem as horrible because we forget them as we stay in the present moment. As we grow older these episodes have a way of rearing their heads so we can examine them and release the fears and traumas with the maturity that we now have.

My tonsils and adenoids were removed when I was seven or eight years old. In those days, it was a common occurrence. I went to the hospital and that in itself was a big deal; it was rare to go to the hospital unless you were dying. I was so very, very scared. I remember my Mom coming into my hospital room after the surgery with a present for me. It was a doll. I had not had a doll until that point in time.

Oh, how I loved that doll. I finally had a baby of my own. It had a hard head and the hands and feet were hard but the rest of the body was stuffed, making it soft to hold. I spent hours playing dolls, house, and dress up, by myself and with my girlfriends.

Once I dropped my doll on the sidewalk and she was left with a big hole in her head. I was crushed and cried heartbrokenly. I tried to fix the hole with tape but it was too big. My mom soothed me and made my doll a lot of bonnets to cover my mishap.

One day, I realized that my doll was missing. I could find her nowhere. I searched and I searched and asked everyone in the family if they had seen her but no one had. I felt like my child was missing. I was despondent for days and it was hard to console me.

Years later, I was told that Andy had decided I did not need it anymore and he threw it into the furnace of the front house. He felt like it was time I grew up and stopped playing with dolls.

When you are a girl child, your doll is your most prized possession. At least back then, we girls would generally only get one doll each if we were lucky.

I need to say my father did a good thing. There was a carnival at the church and my father kept playing at something until he won me this huge "new" doll and brought it home for me.

I could not love this one though. It was so tall, half as tall as me, so I could not cuddle it in my arms like a baby. It was not stuffed; it was made of plastic and it was so hard.

Was I being ungrateful, perhaps? But my other doll was my baby and could not be replaced. This new one disappeared too and I was told that Andy was very jealous because my father had spent time and money on me so he had burned that doll in the furnace too.

I remember being a stubborn child. If you asked me for something, I would give you the moon. But…don't tell me I have to do something because my back would go up and I could not be budged. I hated doing what I was told because I had no voice or opinion at home.

I guess I was being a bratty child one noontime. In those days, children came home for lunch. My dad was home and when I did something, I don't remember what, he picked me up and threw me off the porch onto the gravel driveway. I was sobbing, it was so painful. Not just physically but emotionally. I had no choice but to go to school because he told me I had to.

The nuns were the ones who cleaned me up and tried to take all the little black stones out of my knees so they would heal properly. It took a long time for the grit to finally grow out and for my knees to heal enough so that I could kneel in church or when I said my prayers.

I remember one particular day when I was feeling especially pretty. I never had new clothes because I would get all my cousin's hand me downs which were quite nice because that family had more money than we did. In fact, I only ever had two new dresses, one for my graduation from grammar school and one for my graduation from high school.

Anyway, I guess I was about 11 years old and since I did not start my menstrual period until I was fourteen and a half years old, I was built like a boy. I had put on a pair of shorts and a nice white halter midriff blouse with the large white "collar". I came outside and my dad started to scream at me.

He said: "Get in the house you little tramp and change your clothes. Are you trying to tempt the men?"

There were no other men around except him and I did not understand what he meant by tempting the men. I was too young to know about sex and any connotations he was making. I was very self conscious from that point on. I didn't know what I had done wrong or how I could keep from doing it again.

When I was about 11 years old, my girlfriend and I went to a local pond to swim. There were a couple of cute boys our age and we all got along really well. Unknown to either of us girls, my older brother and his friends waited on the path for the boys to leave for home and then they beat them up. The boys were warned to never come near us again.

After my parent's divorce proceedings had begun, my mother placed the responsibility on me to protect my younger brothers. She was afraid that my father would come and take the boys. Not that he wanted them but he wanted to hurt her.

I remember one day when I was coming home from school with William and Charlie and saw my dad in the yard. I took their little hands and we ran as fast as we could away from there.

Where to go? I was so scared that I have blocked where I took my brothers out of my mind even up to this day. We ran away and waited until I saw my mom appear before we dared to come back home.

To this day, I believe that the deafness in my left ear was caused psychosomatically by trying to block out all the abuse I heard at night between my mom and dad. If I placed my right hearing ear on the pillow and I could not hear anything out of my left ear, then I could not hear the sounds and I could fall asleep.

During this time in my life I never questioned why my mom never spanked me. It was later on that these questions brought memories back to me. My mom never hit me but I remember once during these trying times when she lost her patience with me.

I don't know if I was giving her a hard time but I see her and me in the kitchen and all of a sudden she lost it. She lost the temper that I never knew she had. She threw a fork in desperation and it hit my arm and stuck there. I know she did not mean to hit me but it happened. It was one of those moments that are suspended in time. I felt nothing and I just stared at the way the fork was stuck in my arm.

Needless to say, my mother was aghast at what had happened. She kept saying, "I am so sorry, I did not mean for that to hit you. I am so sorry. Can you ever forgive me?" She was hysterical by this time and I had to calm her down.

She dressed my wound and then collapsed on the couch while I put cold facecloths to her forehead trying to soothe her.

Hindsight allows you to understand the lessons and meanings behind what you have experienced. Looking back at my childhood, I realize now that I had been given a great love of spirituality that would carry right through to this day. It was a formation of my character and I really would like to thank all the people who were in this drama with me.

3
TEEN YEARS INTO MARRIAGE

My best friend Rose and I were going to go to high school in Maine where we would be in training to become nuns. However, her mom became pregnant and needed her to go to school locally so she would be able to help with her siblings.

I was in a quandary as to whether I would go away and when I mentioned it to my father; he insisted that I go to school in Maine. He was adamant that I become a nun and his stubborn stance just made my back go up so that I refused. I surprised myself when I finally made the decision to go to a local high school.

I guess I got my stubbornness from my father and he could control me in a lot of ways but this time my mind was made up. My mother even had the courage to stand up for me. Isn't it amazing how an episode like this determines a path in your life? I guess motherhood was to be my true calling.

My dad was crippled with arthritis in his back so he would go off to Arizona for the winter to lessen the pain. He sent us no money or letters; he just showed back up in the spring. My mom was a very naïve woman who saw the best in everyone and it would not occur to her to be devious in any way.

She believed that the man was the head of the household and she was to obey everything he told her. If that meant rape and beatings, then she just accepted it.

When I was twelve, the pastor of our local church took it into his own hands to protect my mother from all the abuse she was taking by helping her get a divorce. Of course my father blamed everything on my mother as most dysfunctional people do. And being a staunch Catholic, he could not believe that the pastor would take steps to break up his family.

The happiest years of my life began after my parents' divorce. I was a teenager and my mom would take me square dancing at the YMCA. She joined a group of dancers who put on exhibits and participated in dance demonstrations at a big fair. I joined the junior dancers and ended up being the lead girl for our group, which was quite a coup.

Before this, no boy would show any interest in me or ask me for a date. I did have one date as a freshman with a boy from my class. I remember taking the bus to meet him downtown so we could go to the movies. My mom did not have her license yet and neither did the young man. We had fun but I never figured out why he didn't ask me out again.

Many years later after I was married, I became aware of my brother Andy's control over the boys in my life. He and I went to the same high school and it took a few years before I realized that my older brother was the reason I was not being approached by a boy. He thought he was protecting me by telling all the guys that they could not date me, and threatening them with a beating if they dared.

While his intention was good, yet what his action did was leave me with an inferiority complex. I thought I lacked personality, or perhaps I wasn't pretty enough. This kept on until the boys I wanted to date were too old for him to bully. It took years of reconditioning my thinking to realize the assets that I do have.

I met some nice young men at square dancing and began dating. My younger brothers would cry, wanting to come on my dates. They could not understand my need to be off somewhere without them. I felt such incredible guilt that I could not be who they needed me to be.

I did not do much dating due to the home circumstances. There was a man, Ted, seven years older than I, who had fallen in love with me. He had a good job, and his own home, and would have given me the world. He treated me like a princess. I dated him for about seven months because my mother kept insisting how kind he was to me, which was true. I appreciated the way he was treating me but I thought he was too old and too settled. I was only 15 years old.

My mother so wanted me to have a better life than she had so she used all her wiles to keep me interested. I felt so guilty when I realized what a hard life she had had and I wanted so much to please her and also put her mind at ease about me.

"No" just wasn't in my vocabulary. Finally I could not take it anymore. I did not love him and could not see myself spending the rest of my life with him.

My idea of marriage was that it was for life. What I remember most about this kind man were his hands; they were old looking and wrinkled, or at least that was my perception at the time. I would shiver inside when he touched my arm or wanted to hold hands. Rationally he was a good match but I believed in love and would settle for nothing less from myself. This was a moment of rare rebellion!

At the time of my entrance into high school, students had only two choices, commercial or classical courses. Once you chose, you were stuck with that decision for the four years of schooling. I was only twelve years old when I went to high school and I really wanted to go further academically so I chose the classical course so I could go to college.

My parents got divorced when I was a freshman so there was no way I would be able to go to college right from high school and I was stuck with my choice of courses for four years.

One good thing about being 15 years old through most of my senior year was the fact that I could not quit school until I was 16. With only a few months to go, it didn't make much sense to quit even if I had wanted to.

My mom had promised each of us children that she would get us a watch if we graduated from high school. Andy had quit school a couple of years before so now it was my turn to be a graduate.

Today I value that watch as a memento of the trust and confidence my mom had in me. It is a Wittnauer wind up watch that cost $70 fifty four years ago. My mom had put it on layaway in my junior year and paid a dollar a week on it until she had it paid for. I realize now how much confidence she had in me. A dollar was a lot of money for my mom back then. She worked two and three jobs to support us and with four mouths to feed, her money was stretched quite thin.

My younger brothers never graduated from high school either although I had tried to encourage them with every enticement I could think of. Formal education is so essential to not only earning a decent wage but to expand their minds about the world they live in. Charlie even lived with me, my husband and my children while he attended school but he was not able to conquer the pattern that had been set for him by his elders.

I could not work until I turned 16 in February of my senior year. I then got a part time job after school for a clothier. I brought home $23 a week after taxes. I gave my mom $20 for board and had $3 left for bus, clothes and treats such as lunch at our local hang out.

My mom had a surprise for me, a new graduation dress. This was to be my second new dress. When I opened the package, I was aghast. It was "cute" but not sophisticated. It was a shirt dress with short puffy sleeves, a belted middle and a full skirt. The design was clearly for a much younger girl and all the other girls would have straight slinky style dresses.

I really did not want to wear it as it was childish, but I did not want to hurt my mom's feelings. I was in such a quandary. Here I was graduating from high school and I looked like a little girl instead of the mature woman I thought myself to be.

My concern for my mom won out and I wore the dress although I was cringing inside. The only saving grace was the fact that I would have my graduation gown on so it would cover the dress, although nothing could cover the "cute" flats with the bows in the front.

I had quite an embarrassing moment pertaining to my graduation. Would you believe I was late for my own graduation? The graduation ceremony was to start in the Church with a Mass. I often wondered if my subconscious fear of how I looked was the reason I was late. I do remember the feeling of fear and of saying to myself, "What do I do? How can I walk down the aisle to join my classmates? The nuns are going to be very upset with me. I will stand out like a sore thumb. I will spoil this occasion for the others."

I did not want to go and be in such an embarrassing position and yet I wanted to be there. I went to the Church with my mom, who of course insisted I go.

Outside of the Church, as I was about to go in, another student from my class appeared. He was late too. Since the boys were on one side and the girls on the other, it seemed to everyone that our delayed walk down the aisle had been planned. We were not as late as it had seemed and we both walked down the aisle in sync to join our classmates.

The angels saved me once again. Hallelujah! I believe in angels and also that we are all angels to each other as we allow ourselves to be used for divine purposes we are not aware of.

My mom's sisters and family were there and she was so proud. She finally had a child who made it through high school. My aunt gave me a silver heart with a cross in the middle that I still have to this day. Mementos are so important. They bring back the memories of good times and sometimes embarrassing times.

I had always wanted a college degree and I knew the only way to advance in this world was to have an education. When I graduated at age 16, I went to work in a factory doing piece work. I disliked it as it was dirty and did not challenge my mind. I began going to night classes at a local community college while I was working at the factory. I was young and naïve and I learned about another side of life quickly in that factory.

As another "New World" to explore opened, I learned my first lesson of life at the shop with an older man complimenting me and telling me what a good worker I was. He was setting me up or should I say seducing me. The angels protected me again by sending a human angel to me.

My supervisor took me under his wing and told the other man to leave me alone and stay away from me. Unfortunately, this other man was a time setter so he set my quota so high that I never made piece work. My hands and eyes are quite coordinated and I am very fast with them. No matter though, with that rate set, I could not make much money.

I am so grateful that my supervisor protected me and guided me to the people I could trust. I learned so much under his wings and he was such a positive role model for me. I felt safe and protected even if I was making less money. I stayed at this job while attending college at night and worked there after I married, leaving just before the delivery of my first child.

There was a bowling alley in our neighborhood with a small food place attached to it. It was a local hangout for all us teens. There was also a jukebox that we could play and dance to. Although I was only 16, I felt years older than that. I had graduated from high school and I was working and going to night school. There was a man who worked at the alleys and my friend took a shine to him. He was older and that fact always appeals to young women.

At that time, I started to smoke cigarettes just to feel older although I did not like the taste. I am chuckling at what we do to ourselves just to prove that we are old enough to make our own decisions. Of course, I got addicted and I smoked for 20 years before finally being able to kick the habit.

Well, this man took a shine to me. I was quite flattered but I thought he was conceited. He asked me for a date and I agreed only because I knew the other girls liked him. That was youthful pride and conceit on my part but after that first date, I realized that he was just very shy.

After dating for a month I told him that I was too young to go steady and that I would like to date other boys. Tears came to his eyes and it touched me so deeply that I continued to date him. Eventually I was bowled over, no pun intended. I fell deeply in love and felt I would be safe with someone older who would protect me and take care of me.

After dating for four months we made plans to get married. I asked my brother Andy to give me away but he refused. He said that he felt that Walt was not right for me. My mom was quite upset and cried. She felt I was too young but she did not say anything about my choice of a mate. My parents were divorced and

I did not know where my father was and I don't think I would have asked him to walk me down the aisle anyway.

I had gotten quite close to the man who did the calling at the square dances and who was also the head of the dance exhibition group. I asked him if he would do me the honor of walking me down the aisle. He and his wife had no children and were flattered that I asked him.

Neither my mother nor I had any money for the expense of a wedding so I rented my wedding gown but purchased my veil. Walt's family paid for the reception and other incidentals. Without the good will and kindness of my in-laws, I would not have been able to have the wedding that every girl dreams of.

Two days before my wedding we were hit with the hurricane of 1955. We had hung my wedding gown outside the closet. That was the only place that was high enough that my gown would not hang on the floor and get wrinkled.

The morning before my wedding, my mother and I woke to see my wedding gown completely stained on one side. The roof had leaked right above the gown and trailed down the right side of it. All the streets were flooded and no one we knew could get to us to help us out. We called all the dry cleaners and finally one agreed to try to get to our apartment to pick up the gown. The angels were with us and they delivered a bright spanking white wedding gown to me that night; the night before the wedding.

All our honeymoon plans had to be changed as many roads were washed out but we awoke to a beautiful sunny day.

At the church as I was waiting with the man who would walk me down the aisle, my father appeared at the back of the church. This kind and wonderful man offered to allow my dad to walk me down the aisle but I refused as the old fear of him welled up inside of me. My dad leaned over and whispered something to me but to this day I do not know what; he had whispered in my deaf ear.

I married my husband after only nine months of dating. I was married for twenty years and I often asked myself if I truly loved him. I do believe it was my yearning for love that gave me the libido that was so powerful. I had no shame in sex; after all we were one according to the Catholic Church.

I spent a great deal of my life seeking love and approval from the opposite sex. The only way I could seem to get it was through the physical act of making love. To me, making love was the closest I could get to the feeling of the heavenly love that I knew was there. True Unconditional Love, though, continued to elude me. Through the physical culmination of sex with my husband, it felt like there were clouds opening into the heavens.

I swear I could hear angels singing and the feeling of being loved was overwhelming. After the culmination, or shortly thereafter, I was brought down to Earth and felt emptier than ever. Yes, the physical love was heavenly but it was still not the love that I was searching for, that I felt was out there somewhere.

Knowing now how much I craved the feeling of love, the only thing that probably kept me from being promiscuous was my upbringing in Catholicism. Of course I married young in order to have that feeling of love which I did not recognize at the time as being dysfunctional.

Here I was married at 17 years of age to a man six and a half years older than I was. Two weeks after being married and living with his parents, I developed a problem. I had such swelling in the vaginal area and was in a great deal of pain. I did not have a regular doctor so through friends, we found a doctor who would examine me.

In those days, you did not make an appointment with the doctor. You went to his waiting room and you took your turn. First come, first served. After a gynecological examination, my first by the way, I was sent home to wait for surgery the next day. My mother-in-law, God bless her, was the one who through the night would put cold compresses between my legs to relieve the pain. I was so embarrassed. That was my introduction to the loss of modesty that females need to experience all throughout their life.

I went to the hospital the next day and again was subjected to inspection by the doctors and nurses. I believe my face was in a continual blush as I felt like a specimen being gawked at. It seems that Walt had been too forceful and a blood vessel had been broken on the pelvic bone and the blood had leaked downwards causing the swelling. The doctor needed to make an incision and let the blood flow out, thus relieving the pressure and allowing it to heal.

Because of the roles played by each person in my life, I was able to accept what Spirit had intended for me. I experienced unconditional love from Jesus, my mother, the nuns, and my friends enabling me to bring that love to my mission of motherhood.

4
JOURNEY INTO MOTHERHOOD

After our wedding, we lived with Walt's parents for six months before moving to our own apartment. I was six-months pregnant when we moved into a three-room apartment with not enough money to even have a furnished living room. Our living room was used as a storage space and my first born, David, slept in our bedroom.

I was a mother at eighteen years of age and despite all the responsibility I had assumed for my younger siblings, I still did not realize all the things that went into being a mother. I enjoyed my pregnancy even if I constantly scratched my stomach as the skin stretched to accommodate the life that was growing in me.

The first time my child moved in my womb, I was transported to a place of awe and reverence. Thus began my deep appreciation of the Divinity of the womb. I would sit and watch my stomach move at every opportunity. My skin is the dry type that does not like being stretched and I had miles of stretch marks which showed just how big I had gotten with child; yet I did not mind. I was celebrating the miracle of conception that only a woman can know. My body was being used for the purpose of its creation, to propagate the human race.

My eighteen-year-old body changed from one of smooth youth and a 22-inch waist to the body of an expectant mother. I went from 108 pounds before pregnancy to 128 pounds six months after the birth and have never been below that weight since.

It is sad that in this country and society that we do not revere life-giving menses. In some cultures it is considered a special time each month that women can venerate their bodies and the divine purpose of femininity. Co-creating with Mother/Father God to bring another soul to this planet is an honor not a burden.

I did not always feel this way. My monthly menses were a sign that I would not bear life that month and it came as a relief. Now that I look back, I really wish that I had taken that time every month to thank my body for allowing me the choice of whether to conceive or not. During the first ten years of my married life, I spent most of my energy trying not to conceive. I was very fertile and just when I was the most amorous, I would have to deny those feelings in order to prevent pregnancy. This is quite comical, as I was pregnant five times in eight years.

My story is the story of every woman, the holder of the most precious temple and the Ark of the Covenant between God and his people. Women have within their bodies an ark that holds the most precious of gifts, the Secret of Life.

A pregnant woman does not have to tell her body all the myriad of details necessary to sustain this minute spark of life. Her body does it automatically. During pregnancy, a woman needs only to love and care for her body and it will nurture her precious cargo to fruition.

The excitement and adventure of my first pregnancy was almost too sacred for words. In the fifties, we had no way of knowing what the sex of our child would be; we were lucky if twins were discovered before birth in those days. That fact gave such an air of mystery to the process.

Of course, we were careful not to get blue or pink accessories. Those colors were given to us as gifts after the birth when we knew the sex of the child. Before the birth, we would invest in pastel colors of light green, yellow and multi colors that either sex could wear. Society made it difficult when it pronounced that only girls could wear pink and only boys could wear blue and it continues to this day. Never the twain shall meet.

During the era of the 50's, there was no such thing as an ultra sound that would give you the knowledge of the sex of the child before birth. There are many good reasons to know. It is more economical to know the kind of clothing to purchase, to know if you will need another bedroom if you already have a child and also to have a name ready for the baby. Today parents do have the choice of whether to know the gender or not. In fact, I have heard from many parents that it is quite difficult not to know because if just one person knows, then it is so easy for them to give away the "secret."

If I were to get pregnant today, I believe I still would not want to know the sex of the child. That mystery is such a special part of having a baby.

When my son, David, was born I felt like I was doing exactly what I was born to do, to be a mother. In those days, they did not send you home with formula. In fact, they sent me home from the hospital with a hungry infant.

My mother-in-law convinced my husband that it would be better for me not to nurse, although my heart was crying out to do so. When she had her children, she did not have a choice. Every capable mother nursed her infant in those days.

It must have been tough for her and she wanted to spare me what she perceived as a burden. I was raised to respect the opinions of my elders and so I acquiesced to the wisdom I felt she had.

The day that I brought my son home, I learned that the bottles needed to be sterilized and cooled, and that the formula needed to be cooked and cooled. My poor son cried in hunger while I went through the lengthy preparation of his formula.

My firstborn had a very rocky start. He spent his first three months crying almost constantly or so it seemed. The doctors said it was colic, but looking back I think it started with him being hungry for such a long period of time after coming home from the hospital.

Sadly, the first child is the one you experiment on. There are no schools to prepare you for parenthood. And…of course, at the age of eighteen, I thought I knew it all. You cannot get answers if you don't know which questions to ask.

I quickly learned that my husband had no patience for a crying child and no inclination to learn how to care for one either. In the 1950s, the mother always stayed home with the child. That was her job - - to cook, clean, and give her husband peace and quiet even if it meant doing all the child-rearing herself.

Once during the night my husband actually got up to feed Dave. When he finally got the baby to sleep he came back to bed. Just as his body was relaxing, the baby started to cry again. My husband swore and I knew that meant he was losing his temper so I got up quickly before he could get his body out of bed. From then on, I slept very lightly and got up when Dave as much as whimpered.

Dave was only three weeks old when I heard him crying very hard. I went into our bedroom and saw Walt spanking him. I was in shock and asked him what he was doing.

He said, "He's crying because he is spoiled. He is only doing this to get our attention." Can you imagine spanking an infant?

That was the beginning of my motherhood training. I did not yet have enough confidence to be who I was and to raise my children with the instincts of my mother's love.

I spent a lot of time and energy trying to have everything run smoothly, keeping the challenging aspects of parenthood to myself. My husband had no patience with the children and I would rather he be angry with me than be angry with the kids.

I did not want to raise my children as I had been raised. How many of us parents want to do better with our children than our parents did? If we do not make those very same mistakes, we make others unique to us. Oh, if we were only perfect parents our world would be perfect, or so we think.

It was when I gave birth to my first child and felt the surge of maternal love for my child that I truly knew the love of Mother/Father God for me. Babies are so pure. They know only unconditional love. They give and receive this energy as a natural part of being. I simply knew that God watched over me just as I watched over my child.

As a mother for the first time, I guided my small child through his own experience on this planet of duality. A child comes into this world with a pure heart and sees all forms of energy that we cannot see with our physical eyes. All things are created of energy vibrating at different speeds; even rocks are made of energy although the vibration of movement is not visible to the naked eye.

Babies are capable of seeing all the various forms that energy takes and they accept it as the norm. They have their own way of communicating with all of it. Have you ever wondered what infants are saying and to whom they are talking when they are all smiles and gurgles . . . even though you cannot see anyone or anything interacting with them?

When a child is born, he sees only what is. He has no judgment or fear, just faith in everyone and everything. He asks for what he needs and readily accepts all the love that is poured upon him. As my first born son grew into a toddler, he began to learn that not everyone responded to his cries, that sometimes life did not give him what he needed or wanted. Even I, with my unconditional love, would sometimes not respond in the way that he needed. Perhaps I did not understand what his crying was trying to tell me.

It hurt my heart as I saw the veils falling over the heart and eyes of my beloved child. As he grew older, these veils started to come down and he began to perceive the world in a different way than he did before. He did not readily accept everyone who came near. He was not as sure of their acceptance of who he was.

He began to learn patience and love of others. He learned not to be selfish because others required some of what he had. He shared what he had and learned that not all others shared with him. He played games that showed his strengths and games where he needed to adapt to another method. He also began to defend what belonged to him and to stand up for himself when a bully would shove him around.

This is a child's beginning experience in learning the basic fundamentals of living on this planet of duality. Earth is a planet of many dualities: hot and cold, love and hatred, male and female, I could go on and on. These are the moments when children incorporate into their essence how to deal with life. Life does teach them and mold them with all the excitement and disappointments that life holds.

5
YOUNG MOM OF TWO

Dave was a year-and-a-half old when his little sister, Sarah, made her appearance. I was thrilled when my daughter was born. I had always loved dolls, playing house and dressing up like a grownup lady and now I had the perfect excuse to enjoy them again. We were quite poor so she ended up wearing her brother's hand me downs. I had one dress for her in each size so I could dress her like a girl when we went out.

I am chuckling now, as I recall how she had no hair although she was a girl. She was bald until she was one year old. People would think she was a boy, especially with her wearing her brother's hand-me-downs. This was before the days of those bands they have now with the cute little bows to show that the baby is a female.

When Sarah was two and three years old, I would try to put her in a dress, but she was always unhappy and uncomfortable. I assumed that it was because she was so used to wearing pants that she felt funny in a dress.

As she got older, she preferred her brother's toys to her own. She did not like dolls, dressing up or anything remotely considered girlish. My daughter was feminine and pretty but she felt more at home in casual clothing. No matter, a mother loves a child for who that child is and not for what the mother would like the child to be.

Yes, I was thrilled to have a little girl. I did not realize how much my own childhood would impact my perspective on having a boy and a girl. I was quite protective of my little girl as I knew how it felt to be the only girl. Dave seemed so much older in comparison to his infant sister. It felt like he should know more than he did and because of that perception, much more was expected of him in terms of behavior.

He was very good to her and gave her pretty much what she wanted. In fact, she would hit him and then scream. I would automatically tell him to leave his sister alone. Because my older brother had brutalized me, I automatically thought it was my son causing the problem.

No one should have a first child without some kind of training; the first is who breaks in the parents. If only there was some way to get the wisdom that comes later in life. There are no classes to teach us how to become a parent. I loved my son so much, too much to allow him to be a brute. My feelings were that I would protect Sarah from that type of interaction and protect her brother from becoming something he was not.

My husband worked nights and would come home around midnight. I waited up for him every night, as he loved to have beer and talk about what had transpired in his day. We would go to bed around two or three a.m. and I would get up early with the children. I kept them quiet, as he would get very annoyed and irritable if he was awakened.

Our apartment was elongated, with the children's bedroom on one end and ours at the other end, with the living room and kitchen in between. One morning I awoke and went to their bedroom. Sarah slept in a crib and Dave slept in a youth bed. We had a gate across the door so he could not get out of the room without our knowing it.

I peeked in and saw Dave holding a long sharp bread knife in his hands. He was using it to feed peanut butter to his baby sister. He had his arms up stretching so that the knife would reach her mouth. She was standing, weaving in her crib and there he was with the knife in his little hands trying to feed her. I did not want to startle him so I calmly stepped over the gate and took the knife. She had peanut butter all around her mouth and not a knife cut or nick anywhere. She evidently was hungry so he decided to feed her. Dave had put his pillow across the gate so he could just lie on it and topple over.

Miracles do happen. There had to be angels around them to protect these young children from themselves! Angels take care of the children when we cannot!!!!

We were living in an apartment complex; in fact they were old army barracks. Can you believe the rent was only $29 a month? Of course the wages were not very high either so the percentage of income versus living expenses would be the same as today.

We chose to live there so we could save for a home where our children could grow up in a nicer neighborhood and attend school. At this time they were too young for school.

With so many families in one building and such thin walls between apartments, the noise level was high and there weren't many secrets. Tenants were always moving in and moving out so we always had new immediate neighbors. The children had many other kids to play with giving them the opportunity to learn the skills of getting along with others.

My first born son was a child who liked animals and was very gentle with his sister and all the other children. Then a bully moved in next door and he needed to learn how to defend himself. He had a hard time with doing that so his father insisted that he defend himself.

He was told to hit the bully right in the face with his fist which would stop all the bullying. It took him weeks to do it but one day as we were going down the stairs; my son did just what his father had told him to do. He punched the bully right in the face. The bully was behind a gate that was up to keep him from going down the stairs. Of course, being only 4 years old, David had no concept that it was not fair as the other boy was behind a gate which prevented him from retaliating against my son.

The bullying of my son stopped but then the reverse started. My son felt the power of standing up for himself so he hauled off and hit every child that did any infraction against him like perhaps accidentally bumping into him.

My son turned into a bully of sorts. Gone was my gentle boy. I certainly wish that society did not tell boys they need to fight and not to cry when they do. I heard these words so often: "big boys don't cry!" As a mother and female, my first instinct is not to hurt and retaliate but to bargain a truce. I guess that used to be the difference between males and females.

We had another family move in whose little boy would stand at the top of the stairs and urinate down on my kids as they were coming up or going down the stairs. That was the clincher for us. We desperately wanted to give our children a better life so we started to house hunt.

We found a house that was within our means but it was not what we had hoped for. It was only four rooms which meant our son and daughter had to share a room until we could financially afford to build a dormer on our house and create two more bedrooms.

The home was in a small town with good schools so the tradeoff was in their best interest. The air was clean and the noise level was considerably quieter. This was a town where they could spend their lives until they were grown. They made childhood friends just like I did and could walk back and forth to school. Busing children to school was not in effect at that time so their lives revolved around a small community.

My son and daughter each got to plant a tree in the front yard. They were planted so after the dormer was built they could look out their bedroom and see the trees.

They had the normal animals that children have: a dog, cat, house broken bunnies, birds, fish and also iguanas. I must say though that the dog, which was a female mongrel and a cross between a German shepherd and a collie, turned out to be my dog. There is usually one person in every home whom the dog prefers although they love everyone.

David always had a soft spot for animals, birds and even insects. His intuition for life itself was quite keen. When we first got our home, our cellar was infested with crickets. I remember him even creating homes for the crickets with bricks and my rags on our driveway even though he was only 5 years old.

When I was a child, I handled grasshoppers but now that I was an adult, I felt differently about touching insects. David would be quite upset if one of the crickets met its demise so I would point them out to him and he would pick them up and give them a home outside.

I was pregnant again with my third child Max, so the room turned out to be a bedroom for three children. It was not easy on any of them to share such a small space. There were a lot of disagreements between them especially when the two older children wanted to keep the little one out of their things.

One day David was in the woods with his uncle when he stumbled upon a hornet's nest. They did not take too kindly to his upsetting their home so they literally bombed him. He was covered head to toe and his uncle saved him by pulling him out of there even at the risk of himself.

David was only seven years old at the time and he was covered with hornet bites. We were rushing him to the hospital when a cruiser stopped us but when he saw the problem, he gave us an escort.

One of the hornets was lodged in his ear, not only causing pain but the drone of the hornet inside his head was very unsettling to say the least. David kept screaming with terror and the pain. The doctors tried to get it out with pincers but no luck. Cold ether was finally poured into his ear which caused the hornet to get even more frantic than he already was. I would have thought that just putting ether on a cotton ball and placing it up to the ear would have been sufficient rather than the insect being drowned with cold ether.

While we were waiting for the discharge papers, Dave was seeing things and being hallucinogenic. He even crawled under the chair the doctor was sitting in, slapping at things that were not there. The doctor insisted he was fine and continued to discharge him.

When we got David home, we tried to get his pediatrician, with no luck. We were guided to a brand new doctor who would make a house call to see what he could do for the child who was walking into walls, screaming for no apparent reason, and even trying to break the thumb off of his father who was holding him.

The new doctor, who became his pediatrician, admitted him to the hospital and kept him overnight for observation and safety precautions. David apparently had a drug reaction to what was given to calm him down and also suffered the hives from so many stings.

After that excruciating episode, he never quite had the trust in the insect kingdom again and I believe it even affected his trust in the animal kingdom. Although the love of nature still remained with him.

There was one Christmas when Dave had a surprise for both his sister and me. He was shopping for gifts when he came across something he was sure I would love. However he knew that if he bought it for me, he would not have enough money to get something for Sarah.

He is a master at creative solutions to problems so he solved that dilemma by putting both our names on the gift. It was a huge picture of Elvis whom I adored but toward whom his sister had no opinion one way or another. It was not something she would want. He realized that I would end up with it anyway so the problem was solved.

He still has the ability to see through all the possible problems and cuts through to the solution while we others just stand there scratching our heads. He cannot understand why we do not see the solution just as clearly as he does and that talent showed up at the tender age of 10.

Of course, he was a normal boy. He never told me this story but I found out about it much later. It seems a boy had dared him to drink river water. It is so difficult for a boy to turn down a dare because that means he is not manly. So of course he drank the river water, not just a drop but a whole jarful. I am thankful that the river water in those days was much cleaner than it is today. He was very fortunate not to have contacted some very serious disease and the angels were still looking out for him. He ended up with a serious bout of diarrhea but nothing that a few days would not take care of. Isn't it a good thing that we don't know each and every thing our children do? I believe that parents would have more gray in their hair if they were aware of each episode in their children's lives. This is also why each person has a different story to tell.

I enjoyed giving to my children and was sad when they were sad. As a disciplinarian, I believe I failed although I felt like I was trying really hard to be a good parent.

My husband would lay down the law and I was expected to make sure it was carried out. Saying "No!" to the children when they got older physically hurt me and my nervous system echoed that fact.

I could say "no" to protect them from physical harm. That was easy. However, if there was some way I could possibly make them happy, I would do my best to have it come about.

Whenever an argument broke out between the children, I was at odds as how to proceed. One of my gifts is the ability to see both sides of any situation. Therefore, seeing both sides I could not choose a side and I came across as indecisive.

We were visiting Walt's folks one day when my oldest child did something and my husband slapped him. My mother-in-law picked up my child to comfort him and Walt hollered and shouted at her so much that he made his mother cry. That was the last time she ever interfered. I tried to tell her once what was going on in my household but she refused to listen and said anything he did was okay so I never confided in her even though I loved her.

I was determined to make my marriage work and after five years of arguments, I finally gave in and did things his way.

Being so young, I made mistakes too. Hindsight is better than foresight. I had been quite ill for the first five years of my marriage so my physical status had much to do with our problems.

I had my first child nine months after getting married and then another child 18 months later. A year and a half later, I had two miscarriages, a womb suspension, an appendectomy and a thyroid operation.

Most of the time I was exhausted and I knew it. I couldn't swallow pills and choked all the time even when I had nothing in my mouth. According to Walt it was in all my head and I was looking for sympathy. My thyroid condition was discovered when I confessed to my doctor that I had eaten a whole box of chocolate candy bars. I was crying as I was deeply ashamed at my lack of control. Once I was operated on, I felt so good. I was not aware of how bad I felt until I started to feel better. I hadn't realized how hard it was to force myself to do things until I felt good enough to *want* to do things.

The reason I could not swallow pills was that my thyroid had swollen inward and was blocking my passageway. Three months after the surgery to reduce its size I began to feel tired again. Walt and I had a big argument as he did not want me to spend the money to go back to the doctor again.

I went anyway and sure enough, it had begun to enlarge again. Since I could swallow normally, the doctor decided not to operate again and gave me radioactive iodine to bring it down to normal. It was normal for one year and then it plunged downwards and became under-active so that it was necessary for me to take supplements which I still take to this day.

My oldest son loved tropical fish. We had a neighbor who had a large fifty-gallon tank and Dave spent as much time as he could over there watching their fish. My heart told me that he would have given anything to have his own fish. My husband did not agree.

He said, "Fish die easily. He is too young to take care of them and they cost a great deal of money."

My heart went out to my son as I could see and feel the yearning he had. My husband gave me a certain amount of money that I had to use for food, clothing and gifts. I did not have access to the household money and I was only given a $2 a week allowance for myself.

I scrimped on groceries, finding the best sales everywhere, and accumulated enough money to buy Dave the equipment and fish for Christmas. My husband did not know that I was doing this as I had been forbidden to even consider it.

Since I knew very little about fish and their care, my neighbor George, helped me and we were able to get my seven-year-old son started on raising fish.

On Christmas Eve, George brought over all the equipment and set it up so Dave would be surprised in the morning. Needless to say, my husband was also surprised. He was so furious with me that he did not speak to me for three months. Can you imagine not talking to your wife for that length of time? He was so sure he was right.

My son and I would sit for hours and watch the fish. We read all about the different fish and their diseases and how to care for them. The different fish fascinated him and I found watching them very relaxing as well as educational. It was thrilling to see how happy he was even if some of the fish died.

My husband eventually conceded that I had been right all along. He never knew how much courage it had taken for me to go against his wishes. My mother's heart would not be denied. Dave had a passion for animals and nature and I wanted him to have every opportunity to experience that side of life.

I remember one episode of defiance to my husband that really shocked him. At the time he was not giving me an allowance so I had no "me" money.

It was time to do our taxes and I was expected to sign the forms that we were filing jointly. When he asked me to sign them, my heart started beating so fast I thought it would explode out of my body.

I took several deep breaths and said, "No!" He was so shocked that I would dare defy him that he was mute. He put the papers away and I breathed a sigh of relief. A few days later, he asked me to sign them and again I refused. A week later he asked for my signature again, and again I said: "No!"

"Why won't you sign these?" he finally asked.

"You get extra money for my signature and I believe that I deserve to have any extra money that comes from my participation," I replied.

I had been living in fear all this time but I would not back down. We finally compromised and he started giving me $2 allowance each week.

Of course it was not enough money for me to go to the restaurant with my girlfriend and have separate orders but we went and split a hamburger and onion rings at Abdow's restaurant. That was in the days of $1 hamburgers.

If I wanted to have a night out with my girlfriends, I had to make sure that the children were in bed and asleep. If not, then Walt would not take care of them so I could have some time to myself.

As I look back, I have a hard time believing that I was so gullible and allowed myself to be so subservient to my husband. I loved him so much that I would have done anything to please him and it took a great deal of courage for me to go against anything he said. Rebelling against perceived authority did not seem to be in my makeup.

My greatest pleasure was derived from giving. I was told that I was not preparing my children to go out into this cruel world. I was called naïve many times. But I believe we create what we think and I preferred to see the good in all. I definitely was optimistic and had a hard time seeing the opposite sides of life.

I remember another time that he took the car keys away from me for two weeks because I came home later than I was supposed to. Does it sound like a parent/child relationship? I believe now that it was but I could not understand that concept at the time. Although I could understand both sides of an argument I did not have the ability at that time to perceive what was right in front of my face. It is difficult to be objective when you are that close to the problem.

He enjoyed being in charge and having authority over everyone and everything and I was happy to have the security that I craved after my dysfunctional childhood. I give these examples just to show how difficult it was for me to go against any authority. Yet I had many lessons on learning to be independent even if I was a naive and gullible housewife. I am grateful for the time that was allowed me to be a housewife and be home with my children.

Of course, when you are dysfunctional, you are not aware of it and so I allowed my husband to be in complete control of our lives. It is only when you begin to come out of that tunnel of misperception that you realize something is wrong. You cannot fix what you don't know is broken so *IN MY CASE* the drama went from bad to worse.

6
MIRACLE CHILD

My children fulfilled me in a way that I took for granted. It felt so natural to be a mother. As I mentioned earlier, I had had two miscarriages after my first two children and I now yearned for another child. Five years after Sarah was born, I told my doctor I really wanted another child although he was advising against it. I told him, "You will have to give me a good reason why not because I seem to be quite healthy now."

Before my pregnancy with my third child, I had this overpowering urge to be pregnant again. It was unrealistic and I was aware, mentally, that I was better off with just the two children that I already had. I physically craved motherhood the way a body craves food. I heard the call from the divinity of my womb, my life's mission would not be denied.

It seems I had the Rh factor in my blood, which could cause problems in my child. I had also had radioactive iodine for an overactive thyroid. Between the two things, my doctor said it would be nearly impossible to have a child that would not either be physically malformed or a special needs child or even lost through a miscarriage.

Once I had my first child, the cravings increased. It made no common sense but that was what I was experiencing. Yet, rationally, I wanted to wait for several years between children. I was very fertile and although we had tried different birth control methods, my five pregnancies were not planned.

Without either of us knowing it, I was already pregnant. An abortion was suggested, but my heart reeled against that. How could I kill my baby? This child was real to me even in the beginning stages of life. Thus began one of the most trying times of my life.

While I desperately wanted a child on one hand, I was, on the other hand, selfish enough to not want the challenges that would ensue if the child was either mentally or physically handicapped. I felt like I would be saddled for life with this responsibility. Yet, I trusted in God. My faith would not let me harm anyone, let alone my own child.

One of my deepest mantras is, "Thy will be done. Not my will but Thine." I say this to myself on a daily basis. Yet, it is one thing to speak it and another thing to act on it. I felt like a heretic. How could I even possibly consider doing something that I knew was wrong? This was a tremendous test of my faith in God.

If I truly believed that God knew best, that he loved every soul, that His will would certainly not harm anyone, how could I even consider doing the opposite? I was beloved by Mother/Father God and so was every other creation. God created this life I carried within my body. How could I decide to end it?

I knew the reality of the people who are malformed or incapacitated in some way and the difficulties of raising such a child. It had nothing to do with spirituality. It was a question I have asked so many times, "How can bad things happen to good people?"

All people come from God and we are all children of God. We carry a spark of God within us regardless if we are considered "good" or "bad" by other people. I had no answer then.

I argued with myself daily, sometimes hourly. I seesawed from being sure that God protected my child from all danger to the reality of a disabled child. There was no contest, but many conflicting emotions. I would do what my heart was calling me to do. I believed that the Holy Spirit would give me the courage to carry this baby.

It would be the longest months of my life.

The doctor was not there when the baby decided it was time to be born. So they anaesthetized me with ether as I had refused a spinal. I knew the spinal would delay his birth and I did not want that pressure on his little head. They just placed the ether mask on my face and I lost consciousness.

In those days, the mother-to-be was alone in the delivery room without any other family members to advise the medical staff of her wishes. There was no one for me to turn to in case of problems.

The medical personnel made the decisions back then (in the days before all the malpractice suits began). I know they made decisions based on what their training and experience told them to do. It was not a malicious decision, and I am sure that the decision was common practice for those times.

This is but one instance of the mother's lack of power in the decision making of bringing a child into the world at that time.

I missed such an important and long awaited moment.

When I came to consciousness, I spent several hours vomiting from the ether. I had so wanted to greet my baby with love and hope, but it was not to be.

When I was finally able to see my son, Max, I immediately checked out all his extremities. All of his eyes, ears, toes, and fingers were there. His skin was perfect. What a relief! I was told it would be a few months before we would know if, mentally, he was all right. Those were long, difficult months during which we monitored every sound he made and every reaction he had.

I put my foot down this time and insisted on nursing this child. The doctor would not give me the go ahead to nurse early in my pregnancy because of the radioactive iodine that had been necessary for me to take for my then overactive thyroid.

I had not had adequate time to prepare my body and did not realize that I had an inverted nipple that did not want to protrude without help.

The hospital let me borrow a pump that worked out fine; however neither the insurance nor the hospital would let me bring it home. I could not get one like that anywhere else although we tried.

After three weeks of struggling to nurse and trying different adapters and pumps, he did not seem to be getting as much nourishment as he needed so I finally gave it up and switched him to a bottle. At least, I assured myself, I had given him as much of a head start as I could.

After the long months of worry about whether my child would be physically or mentally normal, the craving to be pregnant had disappeared for which I was extremely grateful and although I treasured my children, I was finally relieved of that insatiable yearning. It seems I had fulfilled that part of my womb's mission.

One day I went for a walk with my three children and the dog. The older ones were walking and holding onto the sides of the stroller which held the baby. We came to a street so I stopped to make sure there was no traffic. All of a sudden, the dog spotted a cat across the street and sped across right into the path of a truck.

I had yelled the dog's name but to no avail. I could not let go of my kids so I just watched in horror.

The dog survived, thank God, but in her mind she thought I had hit her, as the last thing she heard before she was hit was my voice screaming her name. From then on, she was no longer my dog. She attached herself to the baby and she was his sole protector.

It was funny to see Max go and curl up against her when he had been scolded for something. She was his haven, as he could curl up, stroke her fur and suck his thumb.

I so enjoyed being a mom even if we did not have much money to give them what I would have liked to. I knitted and crocheted, making many things for the infants and then graduating to sweaters for the boys and coats with matching pocket book and hat for my daughter.

I reveled in being a stay-at-home mom. I loved being there when they came home from school and hearing about their day in school and participating in all of their after-school activities. I could be there if they needed an ear and even just a hug.

At this stage in my life, I felt complete. Every one of us has a purpose for being born and my sense of completing that very important purpose had been fulfilled.

YOU
are here because
your mom honored
the Divinity of Her Womb
which contained
YOU.

7
HONORING THE WOMB THAT BIRTHED ME

Parents really need to be united in disciplining their children. I was simply a puppet carrying out my husband's orders and not agreeing with most of his decisions, but I wanted to maintain a united front as I felt that was best for the children. I knew, though, that I did not have much confidence in my own parenting skills. My self esteem was quite low as criticism about everything I said or did had been constant since we married.

I was not a good housekeeper when I married at seventeen years of age. Is anyone at that age? Walt had lived with his parents for 24 years so he was used to how his mom was able to do it all. I tried very hard to become like his mom, she was my role model.

As I look back on those days, I see that I had focused all my energy into my new in-law family, trying desperately to be like them. Their family seemed to be everything I had wished my own family had been.

I am sure my mom felt left out as I listened to all the advice of other people and tried to change myself so I would not experience what she had. I was so young and youth always lends itself to being cockily sure that doing things your way, contrary to what you grew up with, is the smart thing to do. All I knew was that I was not going to let myself do to my kids what had been done to me.

I loved my mom so much but I did not see her as a role model or someone I could go to for advice. On the contrary, I was the adult female in this relationship as I had always been the mom to my mom. She depended on me for advice about my brothers or help in bringing them up. I felt insecure about making these decisions but faked a self assuredness out of my desire to be a support for her.

Yet, all of my life I never felt that I was good enough. I remember making lists and crossing things off as I did them. I attempted all kinds of ways to make myself a better housekeeper and cook. It did not seem to matter as my husband was never satisfied. I remember once making sure everything was spick and span before asking him how he thought I was doing. He went over to the top of the door jamb and ran his finger across which of course resulted in dust. I would never have thought to dust there.

I learned that lesson really well; I never again asked him what he thought about anything I did.

I was married at seventeen years of age to a man who was older than I. In my mind, I was cocky sure I was going to "fix" all the mistakes of my parents. I believed that through our love we would surmount all challenges.

Becoming a mother and realizing the love that a parent has for her child made me aware of the unconditional love I received from my mom. I was also aware of the void that was in me because of my dad's lack of love for me.

Of course, I was ashamed that my father did not love me so I did not tell anyone about the abuse I suffered at his hands. It is one of the best kept secrets by abused children. I did not let it get around that he cared so little for me that I was beaten and belittled. Children blame themselves for not being lovable and that was pounded into me even more deeply by the abuse I suffered at the hands of my older brother.

After pretending that I was loved by my father for all those years, I got quite confused about what really happened. When you lie there is a tendency to believe your own lies.

I remember asking my best girlfriend who grew up with me if my dad actually had beaten me. She was familiar with what had happened. Was I making up that "story" just to get sympathy and attention as my brother had stated over and over? My emotionally abusive husband kept telling me that I was always looking for attention and that I was feeling sorry for myself.

My mind had blocked out the terrorizing episodes of my childhood and I was confused as to what was the real truth. I finally asked Rose when I became a mother myself if the abuse had actually occurred. She told me that what I remembered was the truth; I was not lying about the abuse.

Actually, I had been lying. I had been pretending that everything was all right whenever anyone asked me because I wanted to be seen as worthy of love.

I could not use my parents as role models as my mom was naive and eager to please while my dad had many emotional and physical challenges that created a bully. My dad had been absent from my life for many years and one day he simply showed up at my home. I was flabbergasted to say the least.

No matter who your parents are or what they have done, it is still important for you as an adult to know that they love you. It affects your own self- esteem, your own self image.

So he was back in my life after so many years and now what would I do? I needed him to love me and appreciate who I was. I knew how important his Catholicism was to him and how he based his whole life on his perception of what a good Catholic was. I knew how much emphasis he placed on going to Church every Sunday.

In my mind, this was my chance to prove to myself that my dad loved me for who I was not for what I did. Deliberately, I did not go to Church for a few Sundays while he was staying with me just to see his reaction. If he truly loved me, then he would not push me away from him for only that reason.

Finally he could no longer hold back and he mentioned how I was sinning. I exploded. "Dad", I shouted, "I go to Church every Sunday usually, but I was testing you to see whether your love was based on what I did or on who I am! Now, I know you will only love me if I do what you tell me to do."

After that episode, he seemed to settle down and realize just what he had been doing. We got along much better after that. I had made my point.

My dad tried to help me around the house and I allowed him to do the vacuuming. Did you notice I used the word "allow"? That was what it felt like I was doing; I did not really want the help but did not want to hurt his feelings. I noticed that a lot of lint was still on the rug so when he was not around, I vacuumed it again. He caught me doing it but never said a word to me about it.

I realized then that his eyesight was not what it used to be. He just could not see the small pieces of lint that were left. I wish I had taken that moment to speak to him about it. I had not come into my courage yet so I just let it slide by unspoken. How many times do we let special opportunities go by because we just don't wish to face what they may bring?

My mom and I had a ritual to see who could be the first to wish the other "Merry Christmas." It was a special thing between mother and daughter and sometimes, because of the hubbub of cooking, I would forget and answer the phone without saying it first. It usually started the day off on a very special note.

I called my mom Christmas Day after the birth of my first grandchild. That Christmas morning I had put the turkey in the oven and then called. She seemed to be out of it, not quite there, as if she had just been awakened. I teased her that I had won the contest that year but the humorous feeling was short lived.

She just did not seem "right." I could not put my finger on it but I just knew in my heart that something was not right. I asked her how she was feeling and she responded that she was fine. I could not shake that feeling that something was wrong.

After I hung up, I told my kids that I was going to see their grandmother; she lived about 15 minutes away. When I got there, she was running a high fever and seemed euphoric. There was no pain but she was too lackadaisical. I called my children and said I was bringing Grandma to the hospital against her wishes. We proceeded through the process and she was finally seen by an emergency room doctor. It turns out that she had double pneumonia with no signs of coughing or being congested.

Her insurance would not cover her hospitalization and she begged me to take her home. I spoke to the doctor and the nurses and they agreed that if I kept her in bed, making sure that she got plenty of fluids and her medication, they would allow me to take her to my home.

I called my home and spoke to my daughter. Sarah was adamant that I not bring my mother home as we had a newborn in the house and she was afraid that the baby would get sick. What a choice I had to make. My mom was a poor woman who could not afford the hospital bills and I could not afford to pay for the bills that would be incurred. I certainly did not want my granddaughter Louise to be in any danger either.

What should I do? I could not choose between them, but I had to. These two women were the most important females in my life. It was a choice between the woman whose womb gave life to me and the woman to whom my womb had given life.

I spoke to the doctor again and he suggested that I keep my mom isolated, away from my granddaughter, and the child would be all right. My daughter was nursing Louise, which was a great protection, and children of that age are not susceptible to the germ that caused my mother's pneumonia.

This dilemma was brought to the Divine Feminine when I asked for guidance. I prayed that my faith in Mother Mary and the peace that she transmits would give me my answer. I brought my mom home on that Christmas day much to my daughter's chagrin. Sarah was quite angry with me.

The spare room is where mom stayed with the door closed at all times. I brought up the food and liquid, making sure that all dishes or utensils used were sterilized. I had a bedpan for my mother to use and I handled all of that myself personally so no other person would be contaminated. I also prayed a lot, too, for the safety of my whole family.

What a happy day it was when we were finally able to let my mom come down stairs and be with all of us. The great-grandmother finally was able to hold the great-granddaughter.

We had four generations all together in one house and all of them were female. Every year I tried to take a four-generational picture to commemorate that fact for posterity.

My dad always went south for the winter due to his arthritis, but that year he was still at my house for Thanksgiving. I was in a quandary as I always have my mom for the holidays and I did not want to shut her out. Her boyfriend had always been included but this year I told my mom that my dad would be here and I would rather her boyfriend not come just this year.

This hurt my mom in the worst possible way, although I was not aware of how deeply at that time. I was just trying to have both my parents. My mom was deathly afraid of my dad and deep down I knew it. I guess the only excuse I can offer for myself is that it was so very important for *me* to have them both. I was being selfish as I realize now.

My mom told me to have the holiday with my dad but she would not be coming. I was crushed as I had always had all the holidays at my house with my brothers and my mom.

Just before putting the meal on the table, we each had a task that would enable the meal to be put on the table piping hot. Mom's job at the holiday meal was to make the gravy; she made the best gravy. That Thanksgiving as I was mixing the flour into the gravy, she appeared at my door. I could not stop stirring or it would not have been gravy; it would have been mush. She came to the stove and hugged me, sobbing all the while. I don't believe I have ever hurt her more. Then she left. It was not a very happy holiday although I made the best of it and put on a happy face.

A few weeks later, I tried to call my mom, which I did at least once a week, and the message on the phone said it had been disconnected. Whoa! What was this all about? I called her work phone number and found out that she had retired.

Where was my mom?

I had no idea. Should I call the police? I tried to quiet my mind to think through all the possibilities. I went by her apartment and was told that she had moved.

Since she had moved of her own volition, I could not involve the police. Her friends did not know where she was. I called my brother in another state and he told me he had no idea where she could be.

This went on for three weeks until I finally got a phone call from her. She was living with my brother out of state; he had lied to me. He had evidently convinced her to quit her job and move out to be with him and he even drove all the way to our town just to get her and her belongings.

Now I was furious. I had always been the one in the family that she turned to for help. I had been the adult in the parent/child relationship and she had depended on me for everything; but now it had changed. I felt very much taken advantage of and betrayed.

Whenever my mother had been sick, I was the one who had consoled her. When she had broken her wrist, I was the one who cooked for her, did her laundry and shopping and did all that she needed until her bones were mended. She could not even drive. I was the one who brought her to my home on Christmas when she had pneumonia and incurred my daughter's anger. When her apartment was destroyed by fire, I was the one who got her salvageable belongings and housed her until we could find her another apartment.

How could she just leave her job and this state without even letting me know she was going? She must have known I would be frantic with worry.

I would no longer speak to her when she called. I sat down and wrote her a letter about how betrayed I felt and it was not nice. It was done in a very accusing tone.

As I went through the grieving process and the anger faded, I realized that my mom was very naive. She had mentioned to my brother about my dad and I am sure he convinced her to do this. He had wanted my mom to live near him for a very long time and this was a solution.

This move of hers really made me realize the fear and terror she had of my dad. We can mentally know a fact but it doesn't mean we actually understand with our feelings what someone else is going through. I had been in fear before so I understood fear but I had not been in terror for my life as an adult so I did not completely relate to her fear.

I had been insensitive to her feelings as I plodded along seeking approval from a parent that I had feared as a child.

As I look back on it now, I have forgiven myself for this betrayal. I will never forget the lesson I learned by rejecting the one person in the world who loved me unconditionally for who I was. I fully understand now the need for a child to have the love and acceptance of both parents regardless of what the parent has done to the child.

My mom was the caretaker for her sister who was in a nursing home in another city. Now that she had moved to another state, that task fell on me. I knew nothing about nursing homes so this was my first experience. My maiden aunt was always happy to see me but was also content when I was not there. She suffered from dementia and had been in this nursing home for about three years so it was home to her.

My mom had overseen all the expenses and made sure she was happy. Now that would be my responsibility. Since my aunt was on Social Security, the nursing home took all of her check but gave her an allowance for her personal needs such as clothes, television access and a telephone. As she was about 2 hours away, I visited her once or twice a month.

The nursing home my aunt was in was being sold and was going to be torn down so the administrator asked me whether I wanted them to place her in another facility in their city or would prefer to have her come to a facility that was closer to me. I gave it a lot of thought and decided that since she had to move to another place anyway, I would bring her closer to me so I could see her more often and my children could visit her too.

My aunt was very angry with me as her dementia did not allow her to realize that she was going to have to leave the only place she felt was home regardless. She refused to speak to me or to anyone else. In her mind, I had taken her from her friends and family and brought her to a new place where she knew no one but me.

For five years she did not speak. My family and I visited her more often than before and I was able to keep a better eye on how she was being treated. In her mind, that did not matter. She was still very angry and blamed me for her situation. She was bed ridden so I was not able to take her outside or to any other surroundings. I would bring her an ice cream cone when I visited and it was one of the few pleasures she had.

The staff reported to me that she was refusing to eat. She would just clamp her mouth shut and no manner of persuasion would change her mind. I discovered later from some of the aides that she was choking on her food quite often. I then tried to go at meal time so I could feed her myself and I had no problems.

It seemed that if she was fed too fast, then she would choke. It frightened her so much that she would refuse to allow them to continue. Certain aides could feed her with no problem but there were some who would try to hurry her up and she would have nothing to do with them.

Since she would not speak to me, I had no idea who those aides were. I made repeated efforts to speak to everyone about this problem but it still continued.

The doctor suggested a feeding tube but I adamantly refused. Here was a bedridden woman who could not even feed herself or even take a drink by herself. She had no voice in what happened to her; she was completely dependent on everyone else to take care of her needs. *BUT* she had found a way to have a choice, the only choice she had. She could refuse to open her mouth to be fed.

How would I feel if I had no say at all in anything pertaining to myself? I could not take that away from her. It was the only thing that she had a vote about; it symbolized her freedom of choice. She was choosing to feel hunger rather than allow someone to feed her so fast that she would choke.

Although she did not speak, her eyes communicated much. I could tell when she was content or when she was hurting or upset. I saw her eyes light up when I would visit or when I would bring her ice cream. I loved her so much but was helpless myself when it came to her caretaking.

She deteriorated to a point that she was getting pneumonia quite often. Finally the doctor spoke to me and, in a round about way, let me know that if no antibiotics were given, then she would just peacefully slip into a state similar to a coma where her soul could make the decision herself whether to leave this planet or not. There would be no pain and the final decision would be hers.

When pneumonia reared its head, they would call me for the decision whether to administer the antibiotics or not. It usually happened during the night so I would be waked from a deep sleep and forced to make the decision when I was most befuddled.

When you are waked from sleep by a telephone call, it comes at the very time when you are the least logical about any decisions. Your mind is still foggy and it takes a minute to even get your bearings.

I can't tell you what a struggle that was. I went round and round in my mind and heart over what would be best for her. Here was a woman who was as small in body stature as a child and was "frozen" into a fetal position. She could do nothing physically and was dependent on others for all of her needs. There was no way a miracle could happen. There was no way she would ever improve. I felt like I was just postponing the inevitable. I could not stand the thought of her being in pain so I finally made the decision to allow her Spirit to make its own choice, the choice of staying on this earth or leaving it for a place of eternal rest and peace.

The first time I was called, my heart pounded and it was difficult to speak. I finally told them to let her rest, keep her comfortable but not to give her antibiotics. She recovered and I was relieved.

The next time they called, a month later, I made the same decision. This time her Spirit made the decision to take her home. I cried and cried; I missed seeing her and taking care of her. I knew in my heart that she was in a better place and yet I still missed her independent spirit.

Little did I know that caring for my aunt was practice for me to learn about nursing homes so that when my mother needed to be placed in one, I would have a much better understanding of how to help her.

Every summer before she was diagnosed with dementia and placed in a nursing home, my mom would come to visit me for a month or two. I thought she was able to care for herself so I never gave it another thought if I left her alone. I worked nights so we had the days together and my husband was home in the evening.

I would feed myself and her before I went to work and leave a plate for my husband so he would need only to put it in the microwave to be reheated. Sometimes I left the food in pans and it would only need to be reheated on the stove. I guess I did not do it the same way all the time.

My husband would tell me that occasionally she would mix all the food together when she saw him driving in from work and put it on the stove. She was trying to have a hot meal ready for him and on the table. Sometimes the food was presented to him in a normal manner and sometimes it was like hash. I talked to her about it, thinking she just did not realize how to reheat certain foods. She seemed to understand but still it would keep happening.

Some times she would get upset and accuse me of changing the locks on the doors because she could not operate the keys she was given. One time I took her to her friend's house to visit for a couple of days and her friend called me that night. It seems she was concerned because my mother was not acting like "herself." I brought her home but I still was not putting two and two together.

She was living in an assisted living building. It took a few months before we discovered that she would go downstairs to attend Bingo and then call a taxi to bring her home. She would give him her address so the cab driver knew very well what was happening. He would take her for a ride and then bring her back to the same building she had been in. She would pay him and then go upstairs to her room.

The paperboy started to complain because either she was paying him too much or she would forget to pay him. When he tried to collect, she was adamant that he had already been paid.

My mom was placed in a nursing home after a fall put her in the hospital. She was still living far away from me in another state. She had dementia but was lucid most of the time. At that time in my life, I was working full time and could not afford to bring her back and care for her on a daily basis. She needed to be watched constantly as she was a "wanderer." She would get confused and walk out the doors at any moment.

The doctors did not think it was Alzheimer's as she was not combative. They thought it might be a series of mini strokes that caused the dementia. It was slow in coming and I did not recognize it.

It takes a while for the family of a dementia patient to actually see what is happening. Hindsight is so wonderful. After her diagnosis, I started seeing all these occurrences in a different light. I believe that angels take care of our elderly also, not just our children. I am so grateful to them.

The doctor at the first nursing home she lived in told me that most of the time my mom seems perfectly normal in every way. "If I was a stranger," she said, "I would not think she was a patient."

That was how my mom was able to get out of the facilities because to visitors, she appeared so normal.

I would call my mom every week and she seemed to be so happy. In fact, if I called her around meal time, she would tell me that she was going to her "job" and then hang up on me. It seems the aides were great to her and they allowed her to set the tables for their meals. She considered that her job. She took her responsibility seriously and that came before speaking to me. She had no concept of any other reality.

I learned not to call around meal times and it still makes me smile today to think of how useful she felt. Useful is what most seniors would like to be.

She "escaped" from this facility and it made headlines in the papers. As this facility did not have provisions to contain her, they transferred her to another nursing home that did.

When I visited from out of state, I would bring my mom to the motel's swimming pool which she just adored. I would take her shopping so she could pick out some of her clothes. She seemed to be content. I insisted that they not give her drugs that might keep her from being active and feeling alive. That was not negotiable.

In the meantime, I had researched local nursing homes so I could bring her back to this area. I found two that I approved of and placed her name on their lists. Thanks to my aunt, I knew what to look for.

Mom was on Social Security and each facility has only so many Social Security beds so the wait would be long. If you had money to pay then you would be accepted quite soon. Or if you were in the hospital and you needed a bed, then you would be placed on first priority.

After a couple of years, management in this nursing home changed their views and did not undertake to make people feel useful and independent. I could tell from the phone calls that they were drugging her to keep her quiet and complacent.

When mom started to be drugged, I hounded the homes hoping for an available bed but to no avail. I remember one time I had spoken to my mom and she was so drugged that she was incoherent and could not answer me rationally.

I got so mad at God. I sat down at the kitchen table and pounded it, crying, "I want her here now, do you understand. I want her here now!"

Within three weeks of my outburst, my favorite nursing home called; they had a bed. Alleluia!

I made plans for my flight down and plans for the both of us to come back. When I walked in to see my mother, I could hardly hold it together. She was in a chair with a tray, lined up against the wall with others who looked just like her. She was a zombie and her head was down on her chest.

I made plans to pick her up with her belongings the next day. I hardly slept that night. When I went to get her, they gave me all of her medications. I took them and placed them in my purse. I was not going to argue with them as they had not listened to me before when I insisted that she not be drugged.

We got on the plane and flew home. When we arrived at the new facility, I gave them the drugs I had been given with an order that she not be given them. I knew she would go through drug withdrawal but I wanted to give her Spirit the chance to come back through. Thankfully they agreed with me.

Day by day, I could see the change, the improvement. Everyone at the facility was amazed at the profound change in her. She would smile and laugh with everyone. She had quite a sense of humor.

One challenge occurred. Her roommate was a former teacher who was incapacitated physically but not mentally. She apparently did not think too highly of people with dementia; she thought they were "dumb." Every time Mom would try to come back to her room after walking around, her roommate told her that she did not live there. Mom did not know any better and kept wandering around looking for her room. This went on for three weeks until I discovered the problem. It seems that this woman did this to all roommates who were mentally challenged.

Mom's room was changed and she settled into having a home. I so enjoyed having mom so close by and I visited often. I had learned that visiting at odd times gave you a better idea of what was happening. Having dementia, she could be mad one minute and have forgotten it ten minutes later.

Mom was mobile so I could take her out to eat, to movies, to visit at my home and even to swim. I could finally have her for the holiday meals again. The thing Mom liked to do the most was going grocery shopping. Think about it! Women spend most of their lives grocery shopping so it would be something that they would miss quite a bit if they were unable to do it. To her, grocery shopping was like coming home. It was a familiar place even if the store was different.

8
BETRAYAL OF MY CHILD

My life has been a series of events that, although similar to many women's experiences, is different in many aspects. Even as a child I could not in my heart understand the callousness of people. To me there was only *love* and if you had that, you had all that you could possibly desire. All the physical amenities then would fall into place. It did not matter whether you were rich or poor; *love* was the only thing to seek.

Walt worked afternoons arriving home around midnight every night. Many years I had waited up for him to come home and we talked as he drank beer before turning in. I knew the closeness with him I used to feel was beginning to diminish.

In every marriage, there are good times and there are times that you feel the need to pull away. I knew he had pulled away but I was still hoping and working towards becoming closer again.

Walt had asked me not to wait up for him any longer and I respected his request because I thought he needed some quiet time alone. Never in my wildest dreams did I ever suspect the true reason for his distancing from me. Had I known what was in his heart, I would have left him and taken my children with me even if I had no visible means of support.

When my second child, Sarah, was sixteen, my world fell apart. My daughter finally confided in me that her dad had been visiting her during the night. I could not understand how that could possibly have happened. How could her father violate the love and trust she had in him? He had definitely crossed over the lines of familial love.

It was a Saturday morning and my daughter was having a sleepover at her best friend's house. All of a sudden she came back home and seemed quite upset. She asked if she could talk to me and of course I agreed.

When she told me what had happened with her father, I was in shock. I went into another world, a world of pain and confusion. I hugged her and told her that it would never happen again.

I did not know what to do and I asked her if she wanted to spend the rest of the weekend with her friend at her house. She looked relieved to be able to get out of the house. This had been going on since she was 13 years old. How could I have not noticed? I knew it took monumental courage to tell me what she had just confided in me.

It was late morning and Walt was still sleeping. Our boys were not home at the time. I went in our bedroom, straddled him on the bed and began pounding on his back in a fury, asking, "Why? What did you do? Why did you violate your daughter's trust?" I was hysterical and could not stop crying.

He would not even move. He would not answer me as I was frantically punching him on the back, wanting to hurt him as much as he had hurt her. I pounded his back wildly, releasing all the fury I felt at this betrayal of my child. He did not respond in any way.

I asked, "Did you touch the boys inappropriately?"

He finally responded. "What do you think I am, crazy? I am not a pervert. In many cultures the father is the first man to teach his daughter about the physical act of love."

I could not believe I was hearing this. He actually believed what he was saying. I felt like I was in another world, a world that was insane and my husband of 20 years was the madman.

You think and believe that you know a person and all of sudden they turn into someone you don't know and worse yet, someone with beliefs that you didn't know they subscribed to and that you totally abhor.

He finally got up and we sat in the living room. He tried to convince me that it was a normal thing between father and daughter. He said he had literature where other societies in other times found it to be completely normal and he wanted to know why that practice should be wrong today.

"We just happen to live in a time frame that considers it to be immoral," he said. I kept shaking my head because my mind could not reconcile what he was trying to explain.

My reasoning and heartfelt beliefs were being attacked and I could not make heads or tails of what he was saying. It was like I was in a fog and no words were being said, only his mouth was moving. Was I in a nightmare that I would wake up from?

My baby, my little girl, had been betrayed by the worst possible perpetrator, her father. My heart was ripped apart inside of me and my mother's love was crying out for revenge. I paced around the house trying to put some normalcy back into my brain functioning, into my reasoning abilities again.

I felt like I was in another world, another planet, where sex between children and their parents was normal. Where there was no such thing as sexual abuse. I kept trying to get the cobwebs out of my brain; I just could not wrap my common sense around what I had just discovered.

Where I had previously loved him, now the only emotion I felt now was hate, searing hatred. He had hurt my child more deeply than anyone could have. It was a betrayal at the deepest level of my being.

I had never known what it was to hate, to really hate. Perhaps you have to love deeply before you can feel the opposite as deeply; I don't know. We often say we hate this or that but that is not true hatred at all. All I know is that I was consumed with hatred for my husband.

My whole being was racked with pain that was unbelievable. I felt like the core of me had just been ripped out, without anesthesia.

Love does not hurt you like that. A mother's love knows no bounds. My husband had hurt my child. I realize now that I had not even considered the fact that he had betrayed me and our marriage. If he had had an affair with another woman, it would not have hurt as much as it did when he hurt my child.

It was years later that the realization of his being unfaithful to me and the betrayal of our marriage vows actually penetrated my consciousness. That was how strong my mother's love for my daughter was. I could only think about her well-being.

I walked to Church to go to Saturday night Mass, hoping to find some peace and sanity there. I left during the Mass, as I could not stop crying. I walked to my friend Rhea's house and we went outside and talked. I had to tell someone and she was such a comfort. She could not tell me what to do and I knew it rested all on my shoulders. She agreed to keep my secret until I could decide what I was going to do.

What I wanted most of all was to help my daughter; she was my main priority. I arranged an appointment with our family doctor. Of course, I had to wait until the weekend was over to see him. I have no memory of that weekend. The boys still lived at home so they must have been there. My daughter must have come home Sunday at some time.

This was so unbelievable to me that I kept mentally shaking my head. The first thing I had Walt do was put a dead bolt lock on her bedroom door. He wanted to leave the house immediately and not have to face her. I told him he had to stay until she had all of the anger and sadness out of her.

I desperately wanted him gone; I could not even stand to look at him. I kicked him out of my bed into the spare room. The boys, one older and one younger, were not aware of what happened. I am sure now that they were aware that their parents were fighting but they did not know the cause.

Finally the day came to see the family doctor, to try and make some sense out of my life. Sarah, Walt, and I sat in his office facing him and I cannot say that I felt very comforted or that he in anyway, eased the pain I was feeling or what my daughter was feeling. I insisted that she see a psychiatrist. He recommended one that I could take her to see.

My husband had told her during those three years that I knew what he was doing. Like the child that she was, she believed him, as she had no reason to doubt him. I only wish I had known.

We went to the psychiatrist, with my daughter going in first. She came out and then my husband went in. When he came out, I thought I would get a chance to talk to the doctor so I could figure out what the best course of action was for my daughter.

"Let's go, we are done," my husband said when he came out of the office. "He doesn't need to see you; it was only about Sarah and me."

I was flabbergasted. What about me? I had been willing to wait my turn but I desperately needed to talk to the doctor. How could

I help my daughter through this trauma without some guidelines to go by?

My training since childhood was to obey when ordered to do something and I found myself following them out the door and into the car. I had no money with which to pay for another visit and the insurance was under my husband's name.

I have never been a quick responder to occasions that present themselves. After a while, I come to the realization of what would have been better to say or do. This was an opportunity that I had let slide by. I did not have any money of my own to pay for another doctor's visit as my husband still only gave me a $2-a-week allowance.

I believe my daughter was so relieved that I knew and was doing something about this betrayal that it gave her reason to relax and she did not appear unduly upset to the doctors. This perception of both doctors made their advice to me quite ineffectual.

Of course, she had been going through this stress for three years so it was not new or a shock to her. She was too young to know the ramifications of what had been done to her. Just knowing that I believed her was a comfort for now.

To this day I wonder what would have happened had I been more assertive. Would my daughter and sons have suffered less?

I was on my own as far as making decisions. I still do not know if what I did was the most appropriate recourse or the best solution for my family. It is so easy to second guess yourself when all is said and done. Hindsight makes for great wisdom.

I told my husband he had to stay until I felt that his daughter had rid herself of her anger and disgust. He was to stay in the spare room until then.

This was a big decision which was mine alone. I went to the family doctor again and spoke to him about what had happened. He was a psychologist as well as a medical doctor and had known the family and extended family for many years. He said that he did not believe that my husband would violate another child, that he was very confused with his love for his daughter and had crossed the line. He assured me no other girl would be in danger of him. He also did not feel that Sarah needed any further counseling in reply to my question of what could be done to help her through this.

I prayed hard and long about that decision. Dishonesty was not part of me and I am not a good liar; it shows all over my face. I could not bear to bring any more shame and hurt on my immediate or extended family.

What would be the point of putting my daughter through the ordeal of testifying about what her father had done to her? After my anxiety about my daughter's well-being there came my sons' welfare and the welfare of other children. Why tell the whole world when it would not help another child and only destroy my immediate and extended family? I knew that child services would get involved if anyone knew.

I asked Sarah if she would keep it to herself and not tell anyone including the boys. That decision was the biggest regret I have now. Today I would have made an entirely different one. Of course I am a different person today than I was then.

Sarah was allowed to treat her father in any manner that she pleased. She could be rude, she could refuse to talk to him, and she could even swear at him if that would relieve some of the physical and emotional abuse that she had suffered. However, I also asked her to respect her brothers as they did not know what had happened.

The boys were not told what had happened because I was trying to spare them the pain of finding out that their father, their role model, was a pervert. I know today that the decision I made only made things worse for them.

I was in *HELL*. My husband never apologized, at least to me. I spoke to him only when it was necessary. I so wanted to put him in jail, anything to ease the pain and make him pay dearly for what he did. His parents and family were just like my family, I was that close to them.

How could I hurt them by exposing their son and brother to the scrutiny of the public? How could I allow him to possibly do this to another little girl? Was the doctor right about that?

I told my husband (and he knew I meant it) that if he ever so much as looked at another young girl, I would haul him into court. He would be exposed as a child molester and jailed.

Sarah and I went for long walks almost daily. Although emotionally I felt powerless to help her, I went with my mother's love and let that guide me as to what I could do to help her. I let her talk about what she wanted to talk about. If she did not feel like talking about the betrayal, it was all right. All I know is that I wanted her to be free of all she had bottled up inside of herself for three years. She did not seem to feel the need to talk about it. I still believe she was relieved that her three year ordeal was over and that I had supported her.

My hatred for the man who violated my child consumed me and everything I touched. I had never known the depths of hate before even though I had used those words. I was in the blackest hole you can imagine and the worst thing was that I could not feel *love* as hate was the only emotion that was in me.

This *HELL* consumed me for a year. I operated like a robot, doing all the normal everyday things. I prayed incessantly but could not seem to find the connection to God that I had taken for granted my whole life. I kept asking Jesus to take this burden from me. It was a fire that consumed every waking thought and I could see no good in anything. I was used to seeing the glass half full but was now seeing it as completely empty. If it had not been for the love I had for my children, I would have ended my life.

I hated Walt so much that it contaminated everything and everyone I touched. Love can be transmitted to others when you feel it and so can hate. I never knew that my youngest son thought my hatred was directed toward him.

He was only 12 years old when all of this transpired and that is a very vulnerable time for a child. It wasn't until years later that I found out about his feelings. Hate is such a volatile emotion, you cannot keep it in. I hated myself for hating.

When I was younger I thought I knew what hate was. How easily do we say we hate this or that? Believe me; you do not ever, ever want to feel true hatred. It is like a fire that will consume you and everything that is dear to you.

9
SINGLE PARENTHOOD

I had been a housewife for 20 years and now that my marriage was on the rocks, I needed to find a job so I could support myself and my children. Not having any experience behind me other than factory work, I did not get a very good-paying job. I needed to start somewhere and build experience so I accepted an office position.

That was also very difficult for Max, my youngest son; I had always been home when he came home from school. No longer was I home and now I still had to do all the housework and the million-and-one things that need doing to keep house and raise a family besides the hours spent working outside the home. How I wish I had been able to give him what I had given my other children.

When Dave became a teenager, I entered a realm I was not prepared for. I simply could not comprehend what was happening to him emotionally as he became a young man. My daughter, being only one-and-a-half years younger was not far behind. I had not experienced such a dramatic change during the teen years because of my dysfunctional upbringing and the fact that I married at such a young age. I was out of my element with teenagers and had a hard time being firm with them.

I felt like such a failure. My children seemed to be having so many challenges with which I could not help them. I have since learned that most parents excel at only some of their offspring's different age levels of growth but not at all the ages. Having two parents that are involved with their children is so important because they balance each other out with their different strengths.

A year later I went to a retreat held at my parish Church. It was for five evenings with a priest leading the services. He was such a small man, very diminutive. A small wizened man. I wanted so much to release the hate. I would do anything to feel love again or at the very least, not to feel hate.

On the fourth night of the retreat, as I was sitting in the pew listening to this priest, all of sudden he began to glow. And I mean truly glow. I shook my head, closed my eyes and looked all around but still the glow would not go away. He appeared to be tall and stately within the shimmering light.

The glow would not go away and I thought I was seeing things. I really thought I was going crazy. Then suddenly I felt peace envelop me. I felt something other than hate again; I felt contentment and love. I started to cry, which is not unusual when you are having a spiritual experience so no one seemed to mind or pay any attention to me.

There I was by myself, with no one in particular, but sharing the retreat with my fellow parishioners. I had not cried for a year and here I was sobbing my heart out. In order to be strong for my family, I had bottled up all of my emotions. The cork I had placed inside myself so I would not let out my anger, betrayal and sadness finally popped out and I was free. Free to feel all emotions again.

Words cannot express the release that occurred. I finally felt human again, if that makes any sense to you. I was free to cry, laugh, be angry, smile and be myself. I was no longer imprisoned behind a wall that forbade feeling. I was free! I was free to feel.

I am so grateful for that experience and for the release that followed. I know now that what I was seeing was an *aura*, the living energy which is around everything, even trees, but we usually do not see it. I was given the gift of being able to see the life force around things and I really believe that a veil was lifted off my eyes and heart.

Life is so funny. When I no longer hated my husband, nothing he did or said had any effect on me one way or another. However, I do not condone what he had done; I still feel that it is the worse thing a parent can do to a child, the absolute worst.

Being a Catholic divorce was out of the question, at least for me. By now my daughter was planning on going in the armed services. She wanted this desperately; she had talked about enlisting for three years. The officer asked Walt, her father, to sign the permission slip but he adamantly refused.

My mother's heart did not want her to leave, to go off by herself into the real world. I wanted to keep her with me, both for her and for me. I was not ready to let go of her while she was still so young and after what she had experienced. Her wishes won out, though, and I signed the papers for her when her father refused.

Now that Sarah would be out of the house and harm's way from her father, I could start to think about what I would do with the rest of my life. After the awakening and cleansing that I experienced and with the hatred gone, I could focus on what would come next. I mentioned a separation to my husband and he just laughed at me.

"Why don't you just get a divorce if you're going to spend the money anyway?" he said with sarcasm.

"Fine!" I said.

I can take criticism but when I am laughed at, it just makes me put my back to the wall. I called the lawyer and set up an appointment for a divorce consultation. That shocked Walt, as he knew how much I was against divorce. I came from divorced parents and I had sworn I would not do that to my children.

We agreed to child support for my youngest and what possessions we would share. He wanted to sell our home and I wanted to keep it for a year so Sarah would at least have the knowledge that her home was still here to come home to while she was in basic training. I would have agreed to sell it after a year and split the proceeds.

Walt never thought about anyone but himself and he would not agree to let us stay in the house for only a year. I finally told him that if he did not agree, then I would ask for it from the divorce court. I surprised myself when I had the courage to stand up to him.

Of course, you realize that it was my daughter I was concerned about and again my mother's love gave me the courage to persevere in what I felt was right for my child. He would not agree and so I asked for and got the house with the mortgage still in place.

The first time a young person leaves home is the most difficult. I could not let Sarah go away knowing that her home would not be here for at least her first opportunity to come home after boot camp. It was the only home she had ever known.

When it came to the divorce proceedings, my lawyer knew the real reason for my divorce. As I was not using the real reason, it was necessary to come up with another reason or my soon-to-be ex-husband would have been arrested. That would have been a whole different ball of wax.

I told my lawyer that I would not lie on the stand so he would have to ask me only questions that I could answer honestly. I was physically shaking when the moment came and it was a surprise to me that Walt, my husband, was not going to be allowed to come into the court room while I was testifying.

When I was put on the witness stand, my lawyer came up to the judge and said something in private to him. Although I was asked some ordinary questions, I could not stop from crying or shaking. My divorce was granted and we left. Unknown to me, my lawyer had whispered to the judge the real reason for the divorce so I was spared from more intense questions.

I had no intention of remarrying but I desperately wanted an annulment. Perhaps it was because I needed vindication for what I had been through and I had told no one the real reason for the divorce except for my dear friend, Rhea. I felt like I needed validation. I did not feel I had contributed to the failure of my marriage.

Vows are like promises to me; they are very sacred and I take them quite seriously. I felt like in the eyes of God I would still be bound by my marriage vows if I did not receive the Church's permission to end them. I knew I needed legal permission, a divorce, but that was not as important to me as an annulment.

Annulments do not mean that the children are illegitimate; it only means that the marriage should not have been, for whatever reasons. I did not have the $200 fee for the paper work necessary for the filing of the annulment proceedings.

I wrote to Catholic Charities and explained what I wanted, that my heart really needed an annulment to feel whole again. They offered to pay the money that was needed. I felt part of the load fall away from my shoulders.

Just because I applied did not mean I would be granted one. I knew this. Yet just the fact that they were willing to listen to me gave me a certain sense of peace. I had no one else to turn to for advice or to at least hear my side of the story.

No one can tell me that the Catholic Charities organization does not take care of the poor people. I am living proof that they do. It was not a real physical emergency but it was so very important to my mental and emotional state of being. There is a lot of paper work needed, forms from your priest and your doctor and also from a witness.

Sarah, my daughter, wrote a witness statement for the process. It was important that I have a witness and allow my medical records to confirm what I had written. This part of the procedure is almost like a cross referral. I did not know what Sarah was writing or what the doctors had said. This way the board could see if I was telling the truth. An annulment is not granted quickly or easily; it is a serious step.

Writing the witness statement must have been a difficult thing for Sarah to do and I really appreciated it. I was granted an annulment and felt more at peace with myself than I had felt in a long time. I felt validated and vindicated and free to go on with my life and whatever Spirit had in store for me.

Two years later when I got a job in the postal service which doubled my salary at that time, I took $200 from my first paycheck and sent it to the Catholic Charities. I thanked them for what they had done and asked that they use this money to help another woman who desperately needed an annulment for her own self image.

Sarah left for the armed services and my two sons lived with me. Max was a young teenager, 14 years of age, and Dave was a young man of 19.

I had embarked on a whole new journey with many surprises along the way. Sarah loved the service and when she graduated from boot camp, she offered to pay for Max and me to be at her graduation in another state. That was another world, a world away from all the problems and situations at home. I was so very proud of her and loved her so dearly, yet it was also difficult for me to accept this from my child, as I was still accustomed to trying to help her, not the other way around.

My mother's love is so strong that I am a giver; it is my greatest joy to give. I needed to have practice in receiving though. I now have learned that balance is needed in giving and receiving. If I do not give to myself or accept from others, I will be depleted and then have nothing left to give to anyone else.

When Sarah was stationed in another country, she bought airplane tickets for her brother Max and me to go to visit her for a week. What a new experience that was. I had never traveled so I was not familiar with all that goes into flying and traveling in other circles. I had never left the country and I needed a passport, so another milestone was achieved. I was learning and experiencing so many new things that I had only read about. I was becoming more accustomed to being independent and was gaining more self-confidence. It was wonderful.

I regret to say that my sons did not get along; they fought almost constantly. Dave was trying so hard to be the man of the house, to be the male authority and Max was having none of it. The fighting caused a lot of problems. There were physical confrontations and I was in fear that something terrible would happen to either one of them. Dave was only imitating the parenting skills of his father.

At my new job I was feeling quite insecure and ineffective. I needed so much energy just to do the job well and to learn how to interact in the work place. It was a totally different world from being a housewife and mother for 20 years. I felt like a bird that had been pushed out of the nest, away from the comfort of everything that was familiar.

Max adored his older sister and was crushed when she went into the service. He started having a lot of problems in school, his grades were falling and he would skip school without my finding out about it.

I believe his world had turned upside down and he no longer felt like he had a family. He felt like he had no one to turn to for support and love. Max called me often at work to complain about his brother although I repeatedly asked him not to since my boss did not like his employees taking personal calls unless they were of an emergency nature. Everything felt like an emergency to my young son and I was torn between doing my job and being the kind of mother I wanted to be. My self-esteem and decision-making abilities were at a deep low.

I felt like a failure at everything and could not lift myself up to be the strong motherly image that my sons needed. What could I do? Neither of my sons was willing to listen or compromise. I was in danger of losing my job. With my limited knowledge and experience, my ability to support us and our home was in jeopardy.

Finally I asked Dave, my oldest, to leave the house. Should I say how cowardly I was? I did not have the courage to ask him myself so I asked my youngest brother to come and be with me so I could tell him. My brother told me he would offer Dave the opportunity to live with him. I was shaking so much and my heart was broken in a way that only a mother knows. No mother should be torn between her two sons; I loved them both so much.

I could not financially afford to lose my job and I could not think of another solution that would enable me to be effective at my job and still take care of Max who was too young to be on his own. I felt trapped between two horrible choices. I only wish their father had been able to show his support and love for them and be in their lives.

This decision hurt my eldest son deeply. He felt abandoned and alone. I never thought I would have been capable of hurting one of my children in that way. Unfortunately I really felt that I had no other choice. My son wanted no contact with me from that time on and I could understand how he felt.

Dave had been affected as much as his siblings by the divorce and the ensuing problems. He reacted with anger management problems which caused a run-in with the legal system. As humans, when we are hurting, we lash out in anger. It took a long time for him to learn control but he eventually won out.

My brother William, in Texas, invited Max at age 15 to go out there and stay with them. Oh how I did not want to lose another one of my children!

My heart said no but my mind considered it might be good for him to be away and see another world. Perhaps my brother could be a male role model and Max would have his cousins in the home for companionship.

He was there for two months but it did not work out. My brother was a lot stricter than I had been so the difference was too stark in comparison. It is difficult to adjust to a new environment when your world has turned upside down and you don't know what you are looking for. My youngest son needed more attention and love, not discipline.

He finally called me and asked me to send money for airfare so he could come home. Originally William had driven here for a visit and took Max and his dog back with him, so there had been no airfare expense for him to go to my brother's. However, I needed to take a loan out to get a return airline ticket for him and the dog I had gotten for him at the time of my divorce.

Max seemed sadder and more withdrawn when he came home. I regretted that it had not worked out for him.

Thus began a new chapter in my life. Financially, things were difficult. My employer did not help with my college expenses - - I was attending at night - - so I was on my own. Being a single mother is not an easy job, and with no work skills or background, I had little chance of improving my finances unless I attended college.

I joined an organization for single parents, where I met my second husband. I did not know the world outside of marriage and the world of single people is completely different from being in a partnership.

This organization had a lot of activities for the children and a lot of support for the single parents. Max had felt very different from the children in his school. He did not seem to have anyone to hang around with or who could relate to his situation.

Max seemed to be much happier after we joined. He could relate to the other children about having weekend visits with his dad, living only with his mother and the sudden upheaval of life as he knew it. We went roller-skating, saw movies, camped out, and attended cookouts and a myriad of activities where he could associate with the other children. Although he belonged to a marching band, which was quite active, he still had felt very different from most other children.

Financially it was quite difficult especially since Max wanted to participate in a lot of activities. I used a lot of coupons and sent in a lot of rebates in order to stretch the money further. A boy of 15 does not understand just how tight the finances were.

I remember that I would set a limit to the number of pictures I would take because developing them was so expensive. I was known as the mad camera lady because I had a passion for taking pictures. Perhaps I was trying to capture those moments of joy to look at when I couldn't see much joy in my life at that time.

One time I got the pictures developed and what did I see? Three pictures of a pizza that I had no knowledge were taken. It seems Max was quite proud of a pizza he had made and so he took pictures of it. I guess he was trying to capture a moment of joy also.

I confess that I scolded him severely for wasting the film as I felt that taking pictures was a treat I allowed myself even though I felt guilty when I did. I knew that money used for photos meant that I would have to take it away from my food budget. I wish I had not been so severe and this made me realize that parents scold and reprimand at times because of their own guilt at not being able to furnish their children with the extra things that make life easier.

Max kept spiraling down further and further, and no matter what I did, I couldn't seem to stop him from disaster. He was never happy and always seemed to be discontent with whatever I tried to do for him.

Ever since he was one year old, Max had been a natural dancer with a rhythm that was inborn. Whenever he would hear music, he would dance or keep beat to the music. When he wanted to listen to the radio, he would come to me and click his tongue. The clicking was his way to ask for music; he was too young to speak the words yet.

Max was a gifted dancer and dancing seemed to be his only safe haven. I did my best to keep up with his dancing lessons and the band, going to all of the competitions that ensued. But...it was not enough. I was a working mom now and he could not understand if sometimes, I could not do what I used to do.

He finally quit school at 16 years of age and would not find a job. He was using marijuana and partying with friends all the time although I was not aware to what extent. He begged me countless times to let him go live with his friend and her family. In his eyes, that family would give him all that he was missing at home.

Finally, in desperation, I gave in and allowed him to move out. But he left his dog with me because the family wouldn't allow the dog too. He spiraled down into using cocaine and his dancing was put by the wayside.

Had he had the strength and courage to stay in school and continue dancing, I am sure that he would have been the next dancing star of the world, another Fred Astaire; he was that good.

Again I felt I had failed. For a mother whose heart only wanted the best for her children, I felt that I had let them all down. Years later, Max insisted that I threw him out of the house. Sometimes, for us human beings, memories of a pain remain but the facts do not because the pain is too great. Max did not understand that.

When he was old enough, he joined the Armed Forces. He was trying to follow in his big sister's footsteps. I was quite concerned about how he would deal with boot camp. He came through with flying colors and I was so proud of him. I have never been to boot camp but the discipline and rigidity would be tough on a young boy who had so many inner problems of insecurity.

One day, after about 6 months, he called me and said he was getting out of the service.

"Why?" I asked.

It seems my youngest son was gay and he felt he needed to be honest about this part of himself. Of course they discharged him, but honorably. When he told me he was gay, I started to cry.

He said, "Mom, why are you crying? Didn't you suspect it? "

"No!" I said.

I knew he was a very gentle boy and he felt things deep inside himself that caused him a lot of pain. He was a natural-born dancer so he was teased a lot about being effeminate. But I did not suspect his sexual orientation.

I told him, "I am crying not because you are gay but because I know what the world will do to you. I love you, my son, and that will never change. You are no different to me today than you were yesterday."

A few years later he became a female impersonator. One Halloween he dressed up as a female and he did such a good job of it that he became a lip sync artist. He could imitate all the female movements and looked so much like a woman that he fooled people. He even fooled the uncle he had lived with. At the club that Max was playing, my brother had no idea that the woman making eyes at him and playing up to him was his nephew.

Dave (who was in on the joke) even went up to the balcony and was showering dollar bills down on his brother. We did a lot of laughing over that one.

Max had quite an emotional life, ups and downs; he always seemed to be in drama. He finally met a wonderful young man and they made plans to marry. I was so happy that he might finally have the family that he so desperately wanted and needed.

I got a job at a corporate office and felt like I was on my way to increasing my financial status. While still working for the company, I took the test for employment at the post office. I was on the list for two years and then put in for a year's extension to remain on the list. I was still taking college courses at night.

When my extension for the post office position was almost over and I would have been dropped from the list, thus eliminating my opportunity to work for the Federal Government, I received a call. I was asked to take the training to manually key zip codes at a letter a second. I passed the test in the allotted time and then needed to make the decision as to whether I wanted to leave my office job.

It had been five years that I had been struggling to make ends meet as a single mother. The postal job offered good pay and good security so I chose to leave my office position although I cried all the way to work on my first day at the post office. I was a single mother and needed to consider my financial future so I felt like there really was no choice.

It was necessary as job training for a new postal employee to work the 5 p.m. to 1:30 a.m. shift and also to work holidays and weekends. You do not have a choice as you are locked into that position for a year to fulfill the job you were trained for.

I hated working in the factory atmosphere. A working post office is like one giant factory with all the noise, the machines, the dirt and the clothes that are needed to work in that environment. It is not the post office where you go to mail your letters or packages. This is the one that processes all the letters that have been mailed at the smaller post office facilities.

After a year you can bid on different positions which are awarded to employees according to seniority. But as a new employee with low seniority you don't really stand a chance at getting day work or weekends off. I could no longer go to college at night so for now my college education came to a standstill while a different education began.

What a change that was. I missed the mental challenges of office work and settled into being robot-like. My life at home changed also since my work hours and days off had shifted to working nights, weekends and holidays. Sarah had come home as a single mother to have her baby so she was there for Max in the evenings.

There was a see-through cage in the middle of the floor that housed the time-keeping machinery and the weighing scales. I could see the timekeepers using the calculators and the scales. My mouth would actually water just to get at those adding machines every time I passed that cage. I am very numerically oriented and that was such a magnet for me.

After a year of being locked on the machine keying zip codes, I was allowed to bid on any position. However, one generally got a new position by having the most seniority. As a new postal employee I did not have any seniority at all so had no luck at getting another position even after my mandatory year was up.

Fortunately for me, the time-keeper position was a best-qualified position rather than seniority-based one. With a night-school background in accounting, I realized that I actually had a good chance at that position. When one became available, I put in for it and got it. I was still working in the factory atmosphere with the dirt but at least the work I was doing was now using my mathematical skills. I was much more content now.

I let Dave go his own way for about a year and then my mother's heart would not be denied any longer. I phoned him but he would hang up. I was determined that he would not suffer the same fate that my brothers had.

My brothers were filled with so much hate that they even denied their brotherhood when they were in the same hardware store at the same time. My son deserved more than that.

I called him on holidays and his birthdays. I knew he would hang up but I wanted him to know that I had not forgotten him and I loved him still. I sent him cards at those times also.

Every Christmas and birthday, I got him a gift in case he would show up. I could not have him come and not have something to give him. Each Christmas I would pack away the gifts I had gotten for him and I would bring them out the next year. I even hung his stocking every year and every year it would hang there unclaimed.

When I did call him, I would call him from work as that was the only time he was home. It was a noisy work environment and very dusty with all the paper dust. I remember calling Dave for one of his birthdays during all this noise and he answered and spoke to me. He called me *Mom*. I cried like a baby right where I was, on the workroom floor where everyone could see. That was the happiest day of my life.

If he called me Mom that meant that perhaps we could mend the relationship. He still refused my invitations and I did not want to call too often and pester him. I wanted him to come to me when he felt like it was time.

Sarah, with Louise, my granddaughter, lived downstairs from me in an apartment created just for them in the basement of my house. One day before Christmas, I saw Dave as he was going down the stairs to visit his sister. I did not even think about what I was about to do; I only reacted. I opened the door and told him to come and get the gifts that I had been saving for him. He looked shocked and took the gifts and then proceeded to his sister's place for the celebration. I could not believe that I was so bold but I felt relieved that at least he had the things I had been saving for him.

He told me later how shocked he had been that I kept saving his gifts from year to year. He was my son and his gifts and stocking were added to the family celebration every Christmas. Thus began his journey back to the sensitive and caring young man I knew him to be. Never ever give up hope on your children. They will continue to surprise you.

10
MY CHILDREN AS FORERUNNERS

I believe all three of my children are forerunners who show the world a different aspect of what is usually believed to be truth, especially about single fathers and mothers and also homosexuality. Perhaps this is why I felt that my mission in life was to be a mother.

Throughout my sons' and my daughter's childhoods and their maturing, I felt many times that I did not always make the wisest decisions but I know I did the best I could at the time. My heart and my logical mind knew what to do in many circumstances but it doesn't mean I always followed it. Patience is certainly a virtue and so is hindsight. Sometimes I was just in a mood of self-incrimination or feeling inferior and not having the courage to follow my convictions. Even though some of my decisions I regret from the bottom of my heart, my children grew up to be phenomenal adults. I will write about them in the order of their ages.

Dave was the eldest and the father of my second grandchild as well as my third. My daughter Sarah was the middle child and mother of my first grandchild. My third child, Max, had no children but was a foster parent to several children.

Dave was dating a woman and they were serious, but then they broke up. Unknown to either of them, she was pregnant. When this was discovered, they both knew they would not get married but she wanted to keep the child and to my delight, my second grandchild, my first grandson, Brian was born. When I went to the hospital to see him, my heart fell in love all over again. He was the spitting image of his father and that brought back so many wonderful memories.

Thus began Dave's role as a father, albeit a father who did not have much control over what happened to his child. He did get to see him occasionally but he wanted to see more of him. He went to court to get visitation rights and was awarded every other weekend with Wednesday nights also. I did not get to see Brian as often as I would like but treasured the time when I could.

Dave eventually got married to another woman with whom he had fallen in love and my second granddaughter, Brittney, was born. She was so petite and beautiful that my heart was opened wide again.

In the hospital she seemed to be having a health problem so my daughter-in-law asked me to perform an emergency baptism on her. I was honored and pleased to be asked to do this and she came through the problem with flying colors. She was later baptized in the formal ceremony of the Church.

Trouble in the marriage brewed and my son won temporary custody of his daughter when she was only nine months old and permanent custody when she was three years old. This was an unusual reversal of roles as the woman usually gets custody especially of a girl. What a forerunner he is for the single dads in this country.

Dave chose to sacrifice much for his little girl. He was a department manager at a huge chain store and he was required to work on weekends and some nights also. In order to gain custody, he gave up his managerial position and took a clerk position to spend more time with his daughter. A single parent is required to be home with the child on weekends and at night.

I remember one time when he went to pick Brittney up from her mother's home and she refused to give him back his daughter. They both had restraining orders in place so a certain distance was required. He called the police and when they arrived they assumed he was at fault and threw him in the cruiser.

When he was telling me this, tears came to his eyes. He said, "Mom, Brittney did not need to see her daddy thrown into the back of a cruiser."

He was mortified. The police apologized to him but it was too late to erase that image in his daughter's mind. In those days, the men were always suspected of causing any problems that existed.

Dave did the best he could do with juggling two children with two different mothers and all the schedules necessary for everyone to be satisfied. With his limited time and my working nights, I did not get to see as much of my grandchildren as I would have liked. He did manage to have both children on the same weekend so at least the children were together at the same time and they got to experience a relationship as a sibling. Eventually when my grandson Brian was 14 years old, Dave got permanent custody of him.

My son's prize possession was an antique car which he told me to make sure that Brian received in the event that anything happened to him. I think he felt that he had nothing else to leave Brian that would show just how much he was loved and Dave wanted Brian to know that.

I cannot even remotely understand the daily challenges he went through in trying to raise his children with such conflicting schedules.

My daughter Sarah found herself pregnant while still in the service. She had no intention of marrying the father so she asked if she could come home. Of course, my answer was yes. It was so wonderful having my daughter home with me again and we shared much as she waited for her child to be born.

I had just finished my term paper for that semester when Sarah went into labor. My first grandchild had waited until the last of my college homework for the semester to be done before announcing her impending arrival. My first grandchild was a baby girl named Louise. We had many chuckles over the years teasing her about this.

Sarah and I had taken birthing classes together so I would be able to be with her when the baby was born. Problems arose during labor and an emergency cesarean section was mandated. I was very much worried about my daughter and grandchild as I was not allowed in the delivery room.

Because of those problems and the surgery, my daughter stayed in the hospital longer than normal. My granddaughter was a preemie and was jaundiced so she needed to stay in the hospital much longer than her mother.

Oh, to hold that newborn in my arms. I fell so in love with this child and she just wound herself around my heart. Becoming a grandmother for the first time is a reality that you have to experience in order to understand why grandparents will bombard everyone with the daily news report and the pictures of the grandchild.

Ironically, my granddaughter came home from the hospital on Christmas Eve. Although she had not gained as much weight as was required to be released to her mom, the hospital allowed it since it was Christmas. We were ecstatic.

When Louise was two years old, Sarah used her GI bill and attended a local college. She then won a scholarship at a notable college by carrying all A's and B+'s.

She had been living in subsidized housing with Louise after moving out of my home a few months after my second marriage. A few years later, my second husband Sam agreed that we could build an in-law apartment down in the cellar so that my daughter and granddaughter could live with us but yet have their own privacy and their own apartment. It was much cheaper for her financially and we would be upstairs if needed.

It was wonderful to have them so close again although with the hours I worked, I did not see them too much. Sarah set aside time on Saturday night for Louise and me to watch "The Golden Girls." It was a time I treasured as we both laughed at the ladies' antics.

I brought my mom from a nursing home in another state to a nursing home close by so I could keep an eye on her and her care. During that time I also began college again. I did not have a computer or even knowledge of how to use one. I would write all my papers longhand and then Sarah would type them for me on her computer. It was so time consuming and she was inundated with her own college homework.

Finally I purchased my own computer just to do my college work. It was so much easier to correct and amend my school work than using a typewriter. Sarah now had her "own" time back. Thus began my long neophyte journey with the computer.

Carrying all A's she then received a fellowship to another notable college. It meant moving to another state with her daughter and starting all over again. She faced a lot of hardships and overcame them all to do what she loved.

She was a single mom who put herself through college and excelled in a male-dominated area of study. Today she is a professor at a prestigious college.

Sarah and Louise were there for me as my marriage fell apart which gave me much comfort. I was quite scared to stay by myself after overhearing the plans my stepchildren were making over the phone so just knowing they were downstairs was security for me.

My youngest son Max showed another side of homosexuality that most people did not know existed. When he met the man of his dreams, they planned on getting married. Not legally of course but in as traditional a ceremony as could be had at that time.

Each boy (man) asked his mother to walk him down the aisle. The Unity Church agreed to perform the ceremony. The color of their bowties was matched to the color of the mother's dresses. Each man walked down the side aisles on the arms of his mother. It was a beautiful ceremony and it was done in such good taste.

It was my tradition to furnish the wedding candles that would be used for the ceremony. They would each light one and then each would light the single big candle, signifying their unity. I was asked by my son to bless their wedding rings. Although I considered that to be quite an honor, I had a feeling of unworthiness about blessing their rings; I did not feel I was spiritual enough to give the blessing. I went to see my parish priest, as this set heavy on my heart. My priest listened as I told him about my son and his plans.

"I am not asking for permission to be at his wedding. I am not asking if I can or cannot agree to it. My son has felt alone for most of his life and he now has a chance at happiness. With his drug addictions, he has been to hell and back." My question is: "Do I have the right to give God's blessing on their rings?"

I had no idea what I would be told as I did not know how he felt about gay marriages. He could see the turmoil and pain I was in.

"Have you ever considered that God may be using you to bring the Trinity into this union?" he asked. I started to cry in relief; I had never considered that God might be using me for His purposes in this area.

Many of the guests remarked how tastefully the ceremony and the whole affair were conducted. I think most of them were a little apprehensive about a gay wedding.

Max and his partner became foster parents for three years and helped overcome the judgment on gay parents. He was a way-shower for me and for all the people who knew him.

Does it sound like I am bragging? Well, I am! My children faced unforeseen challenges and not only rose to the occasion but also surmounted them. They definitely are way-showers to the human race on how to overcome adversity and bias.

11
TRUSTING IN LOVE AGAIN
A DIFFERENT BETRAYAL

At one of the functions of a single-parent organization, I met my second husband. He was a single father with many children so we had a lot in common. I had no intention of marrying again, but it was so nice to have someone of the opposite sex for companionship.

I was scared to begin again in a woman-to-man relationship. This quote from Anais Nin shows how I felt at that time of my life: "And the day came when the risk it took to remain tight inside the bud was more painful than the risk it took to blossom."

I remember the first singles dance I went to. It was so surreal. It did not feel like I should be there. There are certain ways to act with other people when you are married, ways that are friendly but not intimate. I did not know how to act single and I felt like I was committing adultery. I love to dance and it is second nature to me but I was not comfortable having other men hold me close. It is obvious to all but the newcomers when you are newly single; it shows all over you just by your behavior and your reactions.

A mixer dance is where the women line up and one of the men from the male line takes the first woman in line dancing once around the hall. Then the man leaves his partner at the end of the line and goes to the first of the line again to dance with another woman. I felt more comfortable with that dance and I met many more men that way.

Sam was one of the men I met and after several months of attending the different functions offered, we settled into being a couple. I dated Sam for seven years and fell in love. I fell in love with him because I saw him as such an attentive father. He was always smiling and joking with his children and they absolutely adored him. After my previous experience with an abusive father and abusive husband, I was just melted by his fatherly traits. He was gentle, kind and physically demonstrative. He treated me the way I had always thought a man in love would treat his woman.

Because of my schedule, we either went out dancing or he brought his children to my home when they were not with their mother. My mother's heart went out to his kids; they looked like they needed a mother's touch.

I listened to him as he told me how his wife neglected their children, as she was so busy doing all this service work for others. He said she was into politics and never home. My heart just melted for him and for them. I know his home was quite unkempt and his children always had torn or dirty clothes on but I attributed this to him being a single father with his own business.

A second marriage was not something I would even consider as long as my youngest son was living with me because I did not want him to have a stepfather. I could not put him in a position in which he might be hurt in any way and he did not always get along with Sam's children. I did not feel it was fair to have Max be unhappy after everything he had gone through.

I fell head over heels in love. When I love, I love with all of my heart. I have been called gullible but if I cannot trust someone then I cannot love them with my whole heart. After dating for seven years, we planned on getting married and I wanted all the children to be our wedding party.

Sam desperately wanted to purchase the home he considered the family home that he had lost in his divorce. I sold my home of 24 years and bought his family home and proceeded to renovate it.

During the time we were discussing our plans for after the wedding, his youngest children lived with their mother. It was quite an open arrangement and he never knew when the children would show up. The closer it got to the wedding, the more changes were being made. By the time we got married, he had the youngest children living with him.

The night of the wedding rehearsal came and we went to the Church. I was not aware of what was happening up front as I was in the back of the Church waiting to walk down the aisle. My pastor came up to me and said he was seriously considering not marrying us. I was shocked.

"Why?" I asked.

It seems Sam's kids were on the altar playing the game "Mother, May I?" They were hopping and running around on the altar in complete disrespect for where they were. I was stunned.

They were Catholic and were raised Catholic; I couldn't understand how they could possibly show such disrespect. Their aunt, Sam's sister, was trying to calm them down but with not much luck. Sam, who was near the altar, never said anything to them and did not even try to stop them from playing their game.

My priest eventually agreed to marry us, as he had deep respect for me. Was that the first sign of what would happen to me by marrying into this family?

This whole episode left me very upset and I did a lot of crying when I got home. Sam could not understand why and proceeded to treat this episode lightly. I would not go for the rehearsal dinner as I was too ashamed. Perhaps if I had had more time to absorb what was going on, I would have cancelled the wedding.

I do not react quickly to anything; I need time to digest it and then I act. This happened the night before the wedding ceremony and I tried not to let it affect our wedding day.

My daughter and granddaughter had moved with me so we did have a full house. They only stayed with me for three months, though, and then moved. Sarah did not want Louise brought up with the examples that Sam's children were showing her. My little granddaughter was constantly being told: "Don't tell mommy."

My heart was broken; I did not know what to do. Here I was a new bride with a new house and a new family and my only support was moving out. What had I gotten myself into? How could I have been so wrong about Sam and his family?

Yet I loved him and would try valiantly to make these relationships work. His children treated me very differently once we were married. I was seen as the intruder, daring to be the "woman of the house" in the very space that had been their home with their mother and father.

A word of advice to all women who marry a second time. If there are any children involved, please do not move into the home that your husband shared with his first wife. You will never be the woman of the house. It (the house) belongs to the children and you do not have a voice. The children are used to it being their home and you are looked upon as an intruder. They honestly do not believe that you should have any say-so in how the household is run. For the sake of your marriage, start off with a new house that you can call home and where you can all begin new relationships with everyone in the family.

Three weeks later an elderly neighbor from across the street rang my front doorbell and, when I answered, she proceeded to burst into tears. She asked me when I would clean up the yard and stop all the partying with its drinking, drugs and loud noise.

I said, "Please give me a chance. I have just moved here and I can assure you that all of that partying and noise will stop now that I am here. I am going to have all the junk removed and my yard will be one that you will enjoy looking at from your home."

I kept my word and we would chat once in a while. She was so grateful that I had moved in and she told me her son felt safer about her staying alone in her home now that I was right across the street.

Let me give you a sense of what it was like. First, Sam and I agreed before I moved in that no girlfriends and boyfriends would be sleeping over. I had not allowed that with my own children and I would not allow that with my stepchildren. He agreed and so I saw no problem . . . until I moved in.

His son had his girlfriend, a stripper, living with him in my home. Sam kept saying he was going to take care of this and she would be leaving. I believed him at first but after two months it still was not happening.

Finally I was told that she had moved out, which I believed. Unknown to me, his son had put a mattress in his station wagon and that was where she slept at night with him. Sam had not lied; she had actually moved out but only to the car. Then, before I came home from work, she would go out to his car to sleep. It took me six months to finally put a stop to this.

One of the children's friends was mad at the way he thought I was treating the kids so he thought he would cause damage to something that was only mine. He threw a huge rock at the first new car I had ever owned. It was late at night because I got home after midnight. The alarm was set off and that was how we discovered what had happened. I pressed charges and insisted he pay for the repair of the damages he caused. That confused him. He needed to take responsibility for his actions but could not understand why he should pay if I had insurance that would pay. Needless to say, my stepchildren were quite angry with me.

Without the cooperation of two adults acting with one voice, the children ruled the roost. There were two sets of rules in the house, one when I was home and another when their father was home and I was at work.

The youngest would climb out of his room on the third floor and would do as he pleased all night. It is no wonder that his schoolwork suffered. I was very much concerned over him. I really loved that child and only wanted what was best for him. The tree that he used as a ladder was eventually cut down yet he still managed to climb up and down just like a monkey.

I found out that the boys were smoking pot and doing drugs. Pot was even found growing in our back yard. One day I had a drug dealer pounding on my back door, screaming for my stepdaughter to come to the door. She was hiding in her bedroom. It seems she had broken into his home and stole his scale that was used to weigh the drugs. I was terrified and she was just laughing.

Another time, I had a girl's father pounding on my front door and when I answered, he pushed his way into the house.

He was screaming, "My daughter is here sleeping with your son."

Trying to calm him, I said with assurance, "No, your daughter is not here. Come upstairs and see for yourself."

Guess what? His underage daughter was in bed with my stepson and her friend was in bed with my other stepson.

I had not heard anything nor did I realize that I had unexpected guests. After I talked with the girl's father, he calmed down and agreed not to press charges, as his daughter had done this before.

My crying and fretting and worrying over all this did little good as their father just laughed at their antics. I realized a little too late that my husband loved his children in the wrong way. He allowed them to do as they pleased and set no standards for them to follow at all. No wonder they were so happy. And…I was perceived as the wicked stepmother.

I was learning another concept of parental love. As parents who love their children, you set boundaries so that the children feel secure and safe even though they complain about the restrictions. I had felt that I was too "easy" on my kids but now was realizing that I had set boundaries for them to follow.

Sam loved his children but without teaching them any discipline. They were prey to all of their own whims and open to being preyed upon by the darker side of life.

After my daughter moved out, all of the kids conspired to get rid of me. They figured they could drive me crazy or at least make me think I was crazy. They would move things around and then swear that I had done it.

Have you ever known something to be true, like what you have said or done? You "know" it without a doubt, yet there are five people telling you it is not true.

Your brain first tries to validate what you know. However, when each of them individually claims their "story," a little question mark appears in your mind. You try to adjust your truth but you just cannot; you know what you know. They were so adamant that they were believable.

I began to question my own knowing and truth. After many episodes like that, and you begin questioning everything you thought you knew. I think they call that brainwashing.

They kept telling Sam about all these things that I was accusing them of and they swore they had not done them. I would put something down and then it was no longer there. When I inquired where it was, they would manage to put it back and say I was accusing them of something they had not done. I was being told that my mind must be going.

It reached the point that Sam thought I was cracking up and I almost agreed with him. When I finally discovered what they were doing, Sam just laughed. I felt like I was in a nightmare, one that I was hoping I would wake up from.

Have you ever felt like you just entered a twilight zone where everything you knew and everyone you knew was completely opposite of who you had perceived them to be? This was not a nightmare; I was actually living it while I was awake.

I kept trying to wake up out of this dream that I had stumbled into. I thought I must be in another culture where all the rules of the game are different. In fact, it felt like I was in a movie and on another planet where what was normal was completely opposite of what I believed to be normal.

Does this feeling sound familiar to you? It should, as that is how I had previously felt about the betrayal of my daughter. How had I gotten back into that kind of nightmare again?

I was considered an intruder in that house. It did not matter that I had bought it legally and that I was financially supporting all of them. Sam had never explained to the kids that it was my home and that I had purchased it. I was not aware that they did not know so I find it hard to blame the children now when they were acting out of what they believed was truth.

He had a way of making you believe what he wanted you to believe. He did not lie; he just did not tell the whole truth and left you thinking what he wanted you to think. I really do not think he realized the damage that he was perpetrating; he just considered it to be the way the world worked.

As I look back now, I cannot believe that I stayed with them for seven years. I must be one stubborn person. When it comes to love, I am very loyal until I am proven otherwise. Perhaps my maternal love was so strong that it did not allow me to give up very easily. I have always believed that Love conquers all. I loved Sam and I loved his kids. My mother's love included unconditional love toward all of them even as I tried to set boundaries for them.

Sam had his own business but he was just starting out again after declaring bankruptcy just before we were married. He had not paid income taxes for seven years prior so that was paid so he could begin again in good standing.

Our second Christmas there, Sam wanted his whole family, which included brothers, sisters, nieces, nephews and all the in-laws, to come over for a Christmas Eve celebration. It was a family tradition and everyone took turns hosting it.

I kept being assured that the day of the party they would all pitch in and help me get it together.

The day arrived and one by one all the people in the house left to go their own way. When I mentioned I needed help and that they had agreed to help, they looked at me like I had two heads. Finally even Sam left and I was left alone to finish decorating and doing all the last minute things that a party requires.

I just sat down and cried. I was so disappointed in them and mostly overwhelmed with what still needed to be done.

Then my anger and indignation kicked in. Here I had been doing all this for them and not for myself. I decided that since I apparently wasn't needed nor was my presence required for the family party, then I would just leave.

I left and spent Christmas Eve with my mother. She was very happy to have me even if it took a catastrophe to get me there. I enjoyed it very much, one of the few times I got to be with my mom without all the others around. I did not worry about how the party was going because I knew Sam's sisters would be happy to help him.

Sam convinced me he needed a building to store the equipment for his business. I gave him a business equity loan of $100,000 with my mortgage-free home as security.

Never did I expect the disaster that happened. It seems the bank allowed him to borrow over a half million dollars and never notified me what was happening, or if they did, the notices went to Sam's office and I never saw them. I assumed Sam had been paying back the loan and since it was involved with the business, I never handled any of it. He had his own office in the building and a secretary to handle all the business paperwork.

One day I received a call from the IRS and that was the beginning of my awakening to what Sam had been up to. They informed me that they had put a freeze on my personal savings account at the post office.

"Why?" I asked.

"Because you have not paid your income taxes," was the reply.

"Of course I have; the taxes have been deducted from my pay check. I filed jointly with my husband; he has an accountant and I signed those papers myself."

"They have not been paid," the man replied.

"If I pay you back, will you release my account?" I asked.

"You have more money elsewhere?" he asked.

"Yes!" I replied.

I had a $10,000 savings certificate about 50 miles away that Sam had convinced me to open. I got the name and phone number of the man at the IRS and said I would call him back. I went to the bank 50 miles away and was shocked that Sam had been into that money also. I did not know what to do. I was in total disbelief.

Checking the tax return we had filed did not occur to me as I do not know anything about business finances. After all, if the accountant had prepared them, they must be okay. That was blind trust on my part. But…if you cannot trust your spouse, whom can you trust?

I did not go to work that day. When he got home, I asked him what this was all about.

He said, "I did not steal your money. I only borrowed it and I was going to pay you back."

"There is no one anywhere that would give you a loan without you first asking for it," I said. "You cannot borrow what you do not ask for. Otherwise, it is taken without permission, which is stealing."

I considered it a breach of my trust and wondered how could I ever trust him again? Needless to say, I did not call the IRS back. I had no money to pay them with. Since I worked for the Post office, the taxes I owed had already been taken out of my pay and I had already paid above and beyond what I would owe at the end of the year.

Three days prior to this, I had sent a check for a trip to China. Was it going to be covered? I had started college again a month before and this trip was going to be part of the credits toward my bachelor degree.

I really did not want to go to China; my world had just been turned upside down and I wanted to stay and try to straighten it out. The check for the trip did not bounce and I could not get a refund so I was off to China in two weeks. My heart was not in it and I feared what would happen while I was gone for 5 weeks.

In the two weeks before I left for China, I overhead my stepchildren planning to get even with me. We had phones all over the house and when I picked up the phone to call out, I heard them talking. I was terrified. Were they bluffing, just trying to scare me? I remembered what they had done before when they tried to convince me that I was crazy. I could not believe what I heard and kept hoping that maybe I had heard incorrectly.

During the entire time I was in China, I pondered over what had happened and what would I do now. One minute my mind was made up to stay with Sam and work things out. The next moment I was positive that I was going to leave him. I seesawed back and forth all the while I was there.

I came home and found that my wishes were again ignored so I then made an appointment with my lawyer for advice and to see just where I stood financially. Sam showed up unexpectedly but it was all right with me because he could tell my lawyer much of what I was not aware of. My lawyer suggested a divorce and Sam said to him, "I never meant to hurt the girl," meaning me. However, I could not truly love without trust, so my love for him was gone.

It was time for me to get out of this relationship. I remember coming home from the lawyer's office and Sarah coming up to see how I was doing.

"Can I have a hug?" I asked. I could not even explain what had happened.

In my heart I knew that Sam was a gambler. Although he loved casinos, his gambling addiction was to the excitement and thrill he got by betting on his own ability and perceived superior knowledge to take chances with his business or in creating new deals of any kind. He just loved getting the best of other business men and to feel that he could do better than anyone else. He was always in some scheme that fell apart. My two best friends had been adamantly against my marrying him as they saw him as a con man. Love is definitely blind.

He became a partner with a man whom I had advised him not to go into business with. The man subsequently went bankrupt and left Sam holding the bag. Of course I was not told that Sam had actually become a partner with this man; I was led to believe that he had not gone along with the deal. I only found out things after the fact.

After I came back from China, I wanted to check out all the records at the office myself to see what had been going on. I was going to go to Sam's office to look things over.

He must have gotten wind of my plans because before I could get there, someone had supposedly broken into the office and records were scattered or destroyed. My intuition says that it was an inside job but I have no proof. I could find nothing that was left in the rubble that would help me.

I was still in a state of shock and felt quite dazed by the events. Sam was legally forced to move out even though he did not think he should have to be the one to leave the home.

Sam's lawyer got a court order to force me to allow Sam to move back in. This was done for pure spite. Sam was only allowed to go through the kitchen and up the stairs to his bedroom. I had changed all the locks so I had to give him a new key and he had the freedom to do what he wanted to do at night while I was at work.

I was terrified. I would lie in bed at night and hear his footsteps on the floor above me, never knowing if he would come into my bedroom although he was ordered not to. How could I have stopped him from doing anything he wanted to do? I slept very fitfully as I was afraid to go into a deep sleep.

I started to notice that food was missing although I was not supposed to furnish him with food; he was to supply his own. I wanted so badly to go check his bedroom to see if the food was there but I was struggling with my own sense of honor. If I did not want him in my part of the house, how could I violate his space even if it was my home?

After a few weeks of noticing the missing food, I finally gave in to my curiosity and went upstairs to check out his bedroom. Sure enough, there were bags of food in there.

He had taken a canned ham, canned food and boxed supplies, soap powder and paper toiletries. I was furious and felt so violated.

"How dare he take my food?" I asked myself.

I was so angry and felt so violated that I grabbed the ham and pounded down the stairs and put it back in my cabinet.

Then I started to pace and I mean pace, around my house. I was being torn in two. Part of me was indignant and feeling righteous in taking back the food he stole from me. After all it was only the ham that I had reclaimed; the rest of the food he had stolen was still in his room. The other part of me was saying that one of my deepest beliefs is in treating people the way I wish to be treated. I would not want him to violate my space, so how could I be a hypocrite? I was fighting with my own inner convictions.

So . . . back up the stairs I clomped with the canned ham and I put it back in the bag it came from. I stomped back down the stairs.

I was still not settled within myself.

"He had no right to take something that belonged to me; I had bought and paid for that food with my own money," I thought.

So . . . back upstairs I went and took the ham again and rushed down the stairs and placed it in my cabinet. Then I began to pace again; I seemed to have no control over this pacing.

My mind was in a whirl and my body was reflecting this fact. I was fighting with myself more than with him. I had to live with myself and I was not too happy with me right now. I was doing something that I felt was completely wrong.

I felt like I had violated his space although it was still my space, even if I was forced to let him stay, even if he was stealing from me. I was doing something that I considered morally wrong. How could I live with myself if I did the very thing that I accused him of doing?

After much pacing and soul searching, I finally came to peace with myself. I knew that I could not control what he did but I could control what *I* did. Just because he was stealing did not give me the right to violate his privacy.

So... back upstairs again with the ham, I placed it back in the bag where it came from, closed the door and gave a big sigh. I had won my battle with the demon that had been raging in me.

I could see this scenario as if it were a cartoon, with me going back and forth, up and down, back and forth, up and down with the ham. I started to laugh, big loud laughs. I bent over with the force of the laughter. I was free. He could not make me into someone I was not proud of, only I could do that to myself.

One bright note is that I won first place in a humor contest at the Toastmaster's Club using this episode from the fiasco of the divorce.

After Sam was forced to move out again, I bought a security system and had it installed. I don't know if I was more afraid of that darn alarm or of someone coming after me. The sound of that alarm was terrifying. Of course I set it off accidentally a couple of times. Another belief of mine is that we create what we fear. Since I feared him and his children so much, was I going to create the very scenario that I was trying to prevent?

I do know that if I saw a car I thought was following me after work, I would take another way home. I did not get out of work until 11:30 p.m. so it was always dark. I was always on the alert, constantly looking over my shoulder. I was afraid but I was not sure who I was afraid of more, my stepchildren or Sam. All I know was that I lived in fear for my life and I felt that there was no one to whom I could go for help.

The lawyer representing me was the lawyer who had handled my first divorce and was also the one who had written up the papers for the business equity loan I gave Sam. I vaguely remember him asking me at that time if I was sure I wanted to do this. I loved Sam and I trusted him and with my own lawyer to draw up the papers, I had felt protected even though it was very difficult for me to put a lien on my home, as it was paid for and mortgage-free.

When my lawyer said we were going to the opposing lawyer's office, I was very hesitant. I did not like the other lawyer nor did I trust him. I felt more comfortable in my own lawyer's office. I have to admit I still had not taken control of my life and still allowed others that I saw as more knowledgeable to make decisions for me.

I was so uncomfortable in that office. When I found out that Sam wanted to purchase my home for $100,000 and would go bankrupt if I did not agree, my back went up and I refused, even against my lawyer's advice. They were both surprised but I am not a quick reactor to circumstances and I would not sign the papers.

My thought was: it was putting my signature on the equity loan that got me into this mess to begin with. I will not sign another paper until I have thought about it.

My rational thinking was: how could he go bankrupt if he could afford to give me $100,000? I no longer believed anything he said and I felt he was just threatening me and would not go bankrupt. I refused the offer as my home was now worth $250,000.

Of course, I made this decision not knowing that I owed over a half a million dollars on that business equity loan. I was still under the assumption that all I owed was $100,000. It would be six months down the road before I would find out just what I owed. My thought was that I could get a mortgage for that amount.

I remember when the lawyer from the bank that was holding the equity loan called me to pay the loan. I told him I was going to get a mortgage for $100,000 to pay the equity loan and wondered if his bank would be interested in giving me one.

"Lady, are you crazy? You owe us over a half a million dollars!" he said.

I was in such disbelief that I could not speak. He was very curt and said he would be filing papers to take my home and I would receive them in the mail shortly. I think I have blocked a lot from my mind because to remember all I was feeling was too overwhelming. I disassociate when I am completely overwhelmed.

A few years later I was asked by a friend if I had ever checked with the bank's lawyer as to how they could allow him to borrow such an amount. My home was not worth over a half a million dollars so there was no equity to cover the increased amount of the business equity loan. It never occurred to me to ask because I was running on pure fear. Fear of lawyers and the terror of losing my home and all that I had worked for my whole life.

How could they take my home? I had done nothing wrong and now they were foreclosing. My mind could not and would not process this series of events. Perhaps it is just as well that much of my day-to-day memory of that period is hidden from my recollection, although I wonder now just how the bank could increase the amount they loaned when I had signed for only a certain amount. It never even occurred to me to question my own lawyer about this fact but I was starting to get very uncomfortable with all this legal stuff.

My lawyer finally said he could not represent me because he had also represented Sam in some legal work. I was given two new lawyers and had to trust them to handle all of my affairs. Perhaps my antennae of suspicion were up because I was having trouble trusting anyone including myself. One day on the phone I was asked by the new lawyers how I was feeling.

I replied, "Do you really want to know how I am feeling? Do you really want to know?"

"Yes," the lawyer answered.

I replied, "I feel like Sam is raping me and you are holding me down so he can do it!"

Needless to say, they no longer wanted to represent me and I was left to find an attorney on my own. It is one of my regrets that I was not rational enough at the time to handle what was happening to me and I was running on pure emotion. I was not a very good candidate to represent as I was very bitter and naive.

Finally I found a lawyer that could represent me. She and I were showing up at court and Sam and his lawyer were not. I finally discovered that she was friends with Sam's lawyer and was doing a poor job of representing me. I think she was inclined not to face her friend with what was going on.

My search for a lawyer began again and the only lawyer that would handle my case was quite expensive by my standards. Of course I was not very familiar with lawyers and what they charge. Because Sam was going bankrupt, I needed to hire a bankruptcy attorney also, which doubled the cost of my divorce.

My new lawyer was a female and she was fantastic. I finally felt I had found someone who could understand where I was coming from. She was great with quick answers and decisions. I would have liked to see her in court on a cross examination, she was that good.

My husband's lawyer, a few years later, asked me why I did not accept Sam's proposal.

I replied, "It did not make sense to me that if he could afford to give me $100,000 then how could he go bankrupt? I figured he was manipulating me again. I did not know at that time that the loan was for over a half a million dollars or I just might have taken you up on it."

"Why do you care if he got the money from the Mafia?" he said.

Sam got away with not showing up for the court dates and his expense sheet was a farce. It was even written in pencil. I had no proof but this remark really made me think twice. Boy, had I been gullible!

After Sam had moved out the second time and before I had the alarm installed, I received a call at work that he was taking the living room furniture out of the house. I rushed home, the only work time I missed in all of this chaos but I was too late.

He had taken it from my home and the police could do nothing because they said it was a marital home so it was legal. My granddaughter discovered later that Sam had taken it to his girlfriend's house.

That's right, we had only been separated a few months and he already had a girlfriend and was living with her. My daughter told my granddaughter not to tell me because she wrongly assumed that it would upset me further if I knew where my furniture really was.

Sam and I were at a meeting with our lawyers when he had the audacity to request that he be able to deduct half of my donations on his income tax return. I was surprised that he was filing. I believed in donating to needy organizations but he disagreed. He felt like we should use the money for ourselves. With that request, I think his true colors showed themselves to everyone present.

12
WISDOM COMES AT A HIGH PRICE

A few years before, unbeknownst to me, while I was still married to Sam, my daughter was going for mental counseling about the abuse she had suffered previously. She never shared this fact with me until years later. This was happening while she was living downstairs in the apartment I had created for her and my granddaughter. I knew our relationship was changing and she was pulling away emotionally as well as physically. I attributed it to my state of being that was so affected by the emotional experiences in my second marriage.

Sarah did mention one time that someone once asked her if she was angry with me for not protecting her. At the time, she said, "Of course not!" Now I believe it must have been someone in a support group she was going to and it had planted a seed in her mind.

It seems that most victims of sexual abuse are quite angry with the innocent parent for not protecting them. I was touched that she believed that I knew nothing but still….there was a void occurring between us.

She had her dad visit and she visited him. They took my granddaughter to visit parks and playgrounds and out to eat. I could not understand how she could even look at him, never mind letting her daughter be close to the man who violated her. She assured me that her father would never be left alone with my granddaughter but I was still full of worry. I still carried the guilt that I had been unable to protect her, as I had never even considered the possibility of what happened.

If I could not protect her, how could she protect her daughter Louise, especially as she was refusing to even consider that possibility? She was as blind as I had been except it *HAD* happened to her with her father as perpetrator. She was forewarned but she chose to deny the possibility that it could happen to her daughter by the very man who had violated her.

I was also hurt because it seemed she was much closer to him than me. I thought perhaps she was belatedly going through the teen years where you separate emotionally from your parents in order to learn who you truly are. Her three early teen years were definitely stunted by the abuse she suffered so I attributed her withdrawal from me as a period that she needed to go through.

Even with that assumption, it did not stop the hurt and betrayal that I was feeling. I felt like I was being treated as the perpetrator, not one of the victims. Every time I saw or heard about his time with them, my mother's heart would break again and the fear would set in. I had lost my best friend as well as my daughter and did not know how to get her back.

A few years ago, I mentioned how much closer she seemed to be to her dad than to me.

She said, "I can relax around him because he is no longer a threat to me. I do not care what he thinks of me."

In other words, my opinion of her mattered and she felt guilty for the void between us. I have always loved her deeply and stood by her but we have not always agreed, especially on the subject of spirituality. She has told me that she is very angry with God.

"If there is a God, how can He allow children to be hurt when He has the power to stop the abuser?"

She had placed the blame on God rather than where it belonged, on her father. She could not face the fact that her father could have hurt her so much. So....she no longer believes there is a Higher Power or God.

My way of coping with the upheaval of my life and my children's was to go deeper inside of myself looking for answers. Ever since I was a child, I have asked "Why?" I know I irritated a lot of people with my incessant questioning and that was about things not as serious as this.

I have always been fascinated to discover and find reasons for people's behavior in certain circumstances. Perhaps it is my way to find the answers so I could stop judging them and therefore give forgiveness and compassion. I will admit that although I was able to release the hate I felt for my first husband, I never really did like him again as a person. I could never find a reasonable excuse for what he did, at least not in my eyes.

By my delving into my spirituality for answers, I succeeded in alienating my daughter. I felt so alone with my concerns and not having anyone I could discuss them with made me feel even more separate. My faith in God, my belief in angels and the knowing that Jesus and Mary loved me unconditionally were my only solace.

If I so much as mentioned the words angel or God, Sarah would physically recoil from me as if I had hit her with a hot poker. My faith and trust in God shattered any of her faith and trust in me. She felt that I was saying she was to blame, which I was not. I never ever thought it was her fault in any way but she did not believe me.

My daughter was lost to me because I chose to believe in God and His gift of free will. I did try to explain to her that God gave His children free will and could not take it back. He cannot use

His power to go against the will of a person if that person is intent on harm or anything else. All of us humans have a God-given choice to decide what we will do. He gave us this power and cannot and will not take that gift back.

This beloved planet Earth is an opportunity for us humans to experience whatever we choose. We do not choose the adverse things that happen to us by other people's choices but we can choose how we react to those events. We have a choice in everything we do, say, think or feel. What a wondrous gift we have been given.

Every person on the face of this earth is treated the same; we are all given the power of choice. If we stop blaming other people or events for our misfortunes and use them as stepping stones to our higher destiny, then we are choosing to accept the sovereignty that was given to us by God. We are His children and therefore we are sons and daughters of a King with the full inheritance of choosing our destiny.

The bank foreclosed - - I lost my mortgage-free home. As a child I was trained to obey the law and even today I have a hard time doing something that is not lawful. I made plans to move and the only apartment I could get by the time the legal paper said I had to leave was in emergency housing. After being a homeowner for 31 years, I was forced into the projects, which are apartments for people with low income. Even so, I was grateful that I had a place to go.

On the day I moved out, I was quite distraught. I felt so alone and helpless. I was 52 years old and all of my savings and investments were gone. What was going to happen to me now? I had always believed that in order to retire, I would need a mortgage-free home and money in the bank. I had scrimped and given up much in order to reach that goal. Now, it was all gone.

As I prepared to leave with the last load of my belongings, I had a great insight. I was angry. Loving makes you vulnerable and I had allowed myself to be manipulated again.

Some men are attracted to hair, eyes, breasts, feet, butts or different parts of a woman's anatomy. Well, Sam was a breast man and wanted me to constantly show them off. I am well endowed but shy about exposing my body. He had bought me a red stretchy dress from Frederick's that he so enjoyed having me wear. I did not enjoy wearing it as it meant men were always looking at me and their wives did not like that fact. I wore the dress probably about three times at his insistence but I was very uncomfortable in it.

It became a symbol for me now of my manipulation at the hands of my husband. I had worn the dress to please him but he had used it to show off one of his so called possessions, me. I went and found two boards and made them into a cross. I slipped the dress onto the short board and nailed the dress by the shoulder seams to the wood. I then nailed the longer board to the railing of the porch on the second floor in front of the house. There my red dress waved in all of its glory.

No one else knew what it meant but he would know: I am not his whore any longer. Now that is what I call good inspiration.

My friend from childhood, Rose, took pictures when she found out what I had done and laughed her head off. It did feel kind of good to make a statement and know that only he knew what was going on.

Although he moved in after I moved out, he had not noticed the red dress waving in all of its glory. When he was finally made aware of it, he was furious. Good!!!

I left the house in much better shape than it had been when I first moved in. All of the rooms on the first and second floor had new wallpaper. There was central vacuuming and a new dishwasher, refrigerator and stove. There was an in-law apartment down in the cellar where my daughter lived; that had not been there before.

The home had a nice paint job and the grounds were all neat with no junk. Even the garage was finally a functional one, whereas it had not been before. There was new paint all over the house compared to the mess it was when I first moved in.

I did not know that Sam would move back in or that anyone but the bank would be interested in it. I had not left any appliances, why would I? I had cleaned out that part of my life and my home reflected that I was ready to move on.

I was told to move out so I did. Sam moved back into the house the day after I left.

He was angry because it did not look like it did when we lived there, I was told. Why would it? I was not going to leave anything for a bank that would not even negotiate with me; a bank that I felt was at fault for loaning him more money than I had agreed on. The bank now owned the house and it took them a year to get him to move out again. He was quite aware of the law and used it to his own advantage.

He lived there rent-free all that time and caused many problems for the bank. However, I can't say they did not deserve it for the way I had been treated by them.

Here I had been willing to repay the loan of $100,000 but the bank chose to foreclose with all the expenses both of the lawyers and of evicting Sam. Then after all that they had to let it go for $72,000 at auction. They certainly did not get their money back and they caused untold grief for an innocent woman who had only loved and trusted her husband.

One goal I had set for myself quite a few years ago was to have enough money to pay cash for a new car and then pay myself back the same amount that I would have paid to an institution for a car loan. That way I would save paying the interest to the loan company and I would gain interest on the money that I was setting aside in a savings account. I had finally done that, so essentially my car was paid for, free and clear.

Sam had convinced me to put the car in his company's name so when my world fell apart a year later, he took the car that was paid for and I had to purchase another car. He was so sneaky, he just took the car one day and I was left with no transportation to get to work or anywhere else.

When I finally located my car in front of his building, I removed my personal items. Of course I could not afford a newer model so I ended up with an older one that had a lot of rust on it and he ended up with a $12,000 automobile, debt free.

My husband pulled all kinds of tricks to delay the divorce proceedings. Court appearances were scheduled and he didn't show up. I had to pay my lawyer for coming to court but having to leave again because of Sam's absence.

In fact, when I was finally granted the divorce, he pulled the same thing again. By this time, the judge was furious and granted me the divorce anyway. I know it was due to the efforts of my lawyer and I am so grateful to her. Thank God that the judge could see what had been happening.

Since Sam was going bankrupt, both personally and with his business, it was necessary for me to hire a bankruptcy lawyer as well as a divorce lawyer just to defend myself. I was advised to go bankrupt but I refused. I have excellent credit. I worked hard for that status even if I have been poor most of my life. Perhaps it was the lesson I learned with being a newspaper delivery girl that instilled in me the value of being honest and truthful.

"All I have left is my good credit and I will not let him take that away from me too," I said to my lawyers. So I did not declare bankruptcy and worked overtime to pay off the ensuing bills. It felt like an eternity before I was free, even if it was only three years.

To pay the $10,000 lawyers' fees necessary to free me from the man who had lied and betrayed my love and trust, I worked seven days a week. I decided if I could work that hard just to pay lawyers; then I would continue to work that hard and begin to make a new life for myself. I went on many journeys that opened my spiritual center to the possibilities of a new awareness (my next book).

I earned my Bachelor of Science Degree in two years as I was going through all the changes of residence and learning to be completely alone for the first time in my entire life. Any money I had had in the bank was gone and the IRS had placed a Federal Tax Lien on me. I was so scared that they would attach my pay, as my job was the only thing that remained.

For five years I had worked with an accountant to get me released from the Federal Tax Lien that had been placed on me. The IRS did not go after Sam because he had gone bankrupt for the second time personally and in business. Supposedly he had no income. Tradesmen like him can work under the table and still lead a very good lifestyle.

Finally my accountant said he could not help me any longer. The IRS was not paying him any heed. I was upset and did not know what to do now. I went into meditation, praying for answers. Suddenly, I heard the word "Congressman." When you hear guidance, it appears to be your own thoughts yet there is something distinctly different in the feeling of that thought.

I have always voted but had no occasion to have any dealings with politicians, but I know guidance when I hear it. I called my Congressman and told him what had happened. I mailed him copies of all the correspondence I had had with the IRS for the previous five years. I also included copies of my divorce papers and Sam's bankruptcy papers.

Within three weeks I had a written letter of apology from the IRS. Yes, a written apology which is framed and up on my wall. Do you know anyone else who has a written letter of apology from the IRS? They also returned my money with interest. I was finally free from the Federal Tax Lien and had also been proven innocent. My good credit rating was mine again.

Miracles do happen, so never give up hope even when it is so dark that no light seems to shine.

I am now able to see how all of these events led me to have courage and stand up for my convictions. I was made stronger by all of these challenges and had more faith in myself. Do not look at your troubles as just devastating events, see them as opportunities to strengthen your own truth and honor the love God has for you so you may love yourself unconditionally.

13
COLLEGE

During my second marriage I had begun college, attending classes on weekends which made me a full time student. I had brought my mom from an out-of-state nursing home to a nursing home close by so I could monitor her health and care. I also went to China for five weeks on a spiritual journey that was accepted for credits by the college. My daughter and granddaughter were moving out of state. All of this had been set in place a few months before my world collapsed around me.

I was not able to get a divorce for several years so there was a span between the foreclosure on my home and the final dissolution of my marriage. Never in my wildest dreams did I expect my life to turn out the way it did in this reality. If I had not lived through this myself, I would have a hard time believing it to be true and not fiction.

Too late I realized that Sam had done to me what he did to his first wife. He lied about her to me and I believed him. Then he lied about me to others. She was no more to blame for their marriage breakup than I was for ours. He was and is a true con artist who can make you believe anything he says.

After having gone through a first marriage that was ripped apart by my husband's betrayal of our daughter and then a second marriage ripped apart by greed and lies, I was ready to be molded.

Like metal that has to reach a certain temperature to be pliable, my reality was ready for change. I did not know into what, as I had lost my home after being a homeowner for 31 years and was forced into emergency housing in the housing project.

Having just started college courses on weekends and making sure my mom was well cared for in the nursing home kept me too busy to have a nervous breakdown. I remember one day in college when the teacher asked me how I was. I just broke down crying right there, right in front of everyone. I could not allow myself to feel self pity or compassion for myself as I would have lost it completely.

My world fell apart and I lost the home we were all living in. It was time for Sarah to move on also as I was forced into emergency housing. She would be going on to a brand new college in a different state. It would be the first time in my life that I was physically completely alone. What a challenge that was and what a beginning to a whole new phase in my life. As I look back, it was Divine Timing (synchronicity) in a sense.

Continuing my college courses after the loss of my home and graduating with a Bachelor's degree during the three year long process of my divorce was part of my awakening awareness of the male domination hierarchy of our day. As I look back now, I see that most doctors were male and most nurses were female. It seemed to be perfectly normal so I did not even question it. But I knew I preferred female doctors because they understood being female and could relate to what I was telling them.

Since childhood I had only known male doctors even though, for the past 20 years, I have asked specifically for a woman doctor.

She has already been through most of it herself, and the physical examination feels gentler.

"The doctor always knows best", is what I had always heard and believed; after all, he was a magician, wasn't he? He knew all there was to know about the body and mind and who was I to question that knowledge and authority.

Over time I began thinking that "old wives' tales" were truer than was ever supposed. I attributed that to my age and my experience as I went through life. But to see it actually written in a book makes the knowledge seem even truer.

The book titled *Clan of the Cave Bear* by Jean M. Auel which was about women in caveman's time and the healing that was taught from generation to generation. It was the women who used herbs and plants to help heal their tribe. This knowledge was then passed down to another female who was trained from youth by the elder female healer. This book impressed me so much that I still remember the feelings it aroused in me as I read it. In fact, I would like to read it again and also reread the sequels.

It constantly amazes me that we do have the knowledge in our heads and the intuition in our hearts, but we are just not aware of it mentally until someone points it out, as in these books. There is usually a reason that things are labeled "old wives' tales" because the female elder held all the keys to healing. The women definitely had the knowledge and experience of healing for centuries. Nurturing and caring for the sick do come natural to the female of the species and so does compassion.

For my college degree, it was necessary to take English courses and one of the books I read for this requirement was *Witches, Midwives, and Nurses* by Barbara Ehrenreich. This book was a tremendous eye opener. I knew that men ruled society, but I never consciously associated the male domination with the medical profession.

One of my college courses was on the religion of witches and I was utterly fascinated by its content. I do not believe that all witches are evil, and I do believe that the moon does have energy that emotionally affects us humans. After all, doesn't the moon affect the tides?

Among religions there are many differences but the major belief in all of them is of a power larger than us and the importance of helping our fellow human beings. I do not believe in annihilating other races or religions just because one does not agree with their practices. If a faction or group of people is harming others, it should be stopped. Reading about the witch hunting from the 14th to the 17th century boggled my mind. That was a tremendously long span to hunt down and annihilate a certain faction of the people. I now realize that the witches did not belong to the upper class but only to the lower class. Poverty forced them to be dependent on each other for remedies and help in entering and exiting this world.

Why is annihilation the only method people in power have to make themselves feel even more powerful? Is their fear of the common people so great?

Can you imagine being afraid to even comfort or aid one of your own family for fear of being called a witch and then be burned at the stake? Talk about oppression!

Children were turning in their parents just for being parents and caring for their needs and wants. Husbands were using this as a way of getting rid of their wives, too. Family and friends were suspicious about every little thing you might do or say. Imagine having to trust no one out of fear for your life. Why are there always dominant males snuffing out lives as in Nazi Germany?

You very seldom find females that are dictators; we are the nurturers. It is time our societies utilize the strengths of both sexes. Male and female were created with differences to bring balance to everything on our planet.

Remedies that the women healers used in earlier times are still in use today. We are even reverting back to many methods of healing that were punishable by being burned at the stake. I like the saying, "Her magic was the science of her time."

Did the Church rely just on the healing from the priests imitating Jesus? What is the difference between prayer and incantation - amulets and medals? I see no difference. It is only a different word that means the same thing.

Today our medical profession is more liberal in allowing females to enter their sacred male domain. Midwives were invaluable to the human race. It's too bad they were female; if they had been male, the profession would not have almost become extinct. Midwifery is on the rise again.

There was such little knowledge about conception and heredity. They believed the man gave everything to the child at conception; women were only the carriers. It must have been difficult for the male to give up his supposed superiority when it was proven that the child was a combination of them both.

I am so glad that the balance between the masculine and feminine is coming to fruition. Our planet and the human race will be the better for it.

14
BURIAL OF THE WOUNDED CHALICE

"I AM THE CRADLE OF HUMANITY... WITHOUT ME THERE WOULD BE NO TOMORROW... NO FUTURE GENERATIONS. HUMAN BEINGS WOULD BE EXTINCT. SAFEGUARD THE CHALICE OF THE DIVINE FEMININE WHICH GUARANTEES THAT HUMANS WILL FULFILL THE DESTINY AND PURPOSE OF MOTHER EARTH," so stated my womb.

I am a descendant of the Ojibwa Indians although I have no legal paper work to prove it. One of their sayings is "Sometimes I go about pitying myself, and all the while I am being carried on great winds across the sky." My new awareness is to be thankful for what I have and to be aware of how Spirit is carrying me.

Menopause came early for me. My monthly periods ended at thirty-nine years of age. Thus I began the journey of menopause and the benefits and drawbacks of hormones. The fact that I had lost my dad a month before and had gotten a divorce from my first husband two years prior after twenty years of marriage was considered a possible reason for my early menopause. In some circles, it is said that a severe trauma will cause it to happen earlier than it would normally.

For five years I was happy not to be "bothered" by my menstrual flow and considered myself lucky to be done with it. I was blessed not to be experiencing any side effects of menopause, such as hot flashes or an inability to sleep.

My physician did not pursue the task of encouraging me to take hormones until a bone scan showed osteoporosis. Since I was menopausal, small-bodied, of white descent and my mother and her sisters had osteoporosis, I was a prime candidate for this bone-breaking disease.

My heartfelt intuition was that I did not have osteoporosis. I had been calling the Love and Light of Christ into my body for quite a few years. I could feel the warmth of that Love and Light and I incorporated that as my signature. Every one of my letters is signed *"Love and Light, Mary Grace."*

While my intuition was telling me that my spine was indeed filled with God's Light, the bone scan, which operates on the basis that the more light it sees, the more porous your bones are, seemed to confirm I had osteoporosis. I could not shake the *knowing* that my body was fine. I really struggled with myself on this conflict between heart and mind.

I talked to many women and researched as best as I could. After five bladder infections in one year, which I was told happened because my tissues had lost their suppleness and pliability from not having estrogen, I finally made the decision to take hormones to prevent the disease from progressing and to offset the debilitating side effects like bladder infections. The vast knowledge of the negative side effects of taking hormones back then was not known.

My body did not take well to them. We tried different brands and strengths but I still did not feel well. I was bloated, despondent, and lackadaisical. The hormones caused intermittent bleeding and insufferable incontinence.

It was the progesterone that gave my body a problem but the estrogen could not be taken alone because of the risk of uterine cancer. Despite the diagnosis of osteoporosis and because of the side effects I was experiencing, I went off and on the hormones over a period of about 10 years. I believe my body was manifesting the push and pull of my mental and emotional indecision of whether I actually had osteoporosis or not.

Something in my Spirit told me not to go the route of hormone taking and, thankfully, I finally listened after doing it off and on for many years. I know my doctor considered me quite stubborn in my refusal to take them. I was leery of hormones and the side effects. Besides that, why would I want to continue having a monthly flow when I no longer wanted to have children?

It seemed that in order to protect the uterus, progesterone was necessary as well as the estrogen. I was told that the only sure way to protect my uterus was to have it removed and I was not a candidate for surgery. My uterus was healthy so this was not an option.

I was in such a quandary. If I did not take the hormones, then my bones would become very brittle and I faced being a cripple for the rest of my life. Yet I was not feeling good about taking them and my body echoed that fact. I was still attempting to follow what my Spirit was telling me but I was not at the point yet of fully trusting what I was receiving as guidance. Oh me, of little faith!

Finally I refused to take any more hormones, thus allowing my body to be natural. I did go for bone scans and PAP tests; I was trying to be practical. For most of my life, I have been called a dreamer because I believe in miracles. I have such faith in the Lord and His Angels. But that faith feels contradictory sometimes.

Finally it was suggested that I have a Vabra test to see the effect of the hormones I had taken intermittently. It is a procedure where the doctor goes into your uterus and takes a piece of it for a biopsy. It is not the same as a PAP test. This is an in-office procedure so it was not a big deal. This gynecologist was new to me but I was not concerned. I lay on the examining table with my feet in stirrups.

When the physician inserted the instrument, I felt such excruciating pain that I moaned, calling out in pain. She quickly withdrew the instrument from me and left the room, leaving me with the nurse. She called for her supervisor, the head gynecologist, and they returned to the room where I was still laying on the table. I was very much confused and questioned what had just happened. The physician left the room and I spoke to her supervisor.

He quickly examined me and explained that the instrument had punctured my uterus because the organ was curved. As they went into the mouth of the womb, the opposite wall was laying on top of it. The test had created a hole but I was assured that it would heal in no time.

I went home and I considered what had just taken place. In the meantime, I chose to see another gynecologist, as I was not confident in the one who had done the test on me. After two years of not feeling well, it was suggested that I have another Vabra test, but in the hospital this time.

They would hospitalize me so they could use anesthesia to do the procedure under more supervised conditions. They were taking no chances this time of puncturing my womb.

The physician said that when she dilated me vaginally and placed the light so she could see, she saw the light go right through a hole in the top of my uterus. So she did not continue any further to take a biopsy.

After the procedure, we talked and she suggested a hysterectomy, as it is unhealthy and dangerous to have an opening into your womb from the abdominal cavity. It leaves the body wide open to the possibility of a dangerous infection. However, the prior gynecologist's supervisor's opinion had contradicted this fact.

I discussed with her the fact that I would want to have my uterus back if I did allow the operation. She balked and said it had never been done. She was very surprised that I would even think of such a thing. No one had ever requested it before so she was at a total loss of how to proceed.

"My uterus has been the part of my body that knew my children before I even physically met them," I told her. "It nurtured them and cared for them while each one was growing into a human baby. Without that part of my body, I would not have been able to have children."

I just could not let them treat it like it was a piece of worn shoe leather and discard it into the heap of throwaways.

Seeing that I was adamant, she finally said she would discuss the situation with some other doctors. It was part of my body and I wanted it treated with respect.

After much discussion with the other doctors, she finally agreed that I could have my womb returned to me as long as a biopsy could be performed to check for any abnormalities such as cancer. I was not crazy about it being cut, but I agreed because, logically, I knew that the procedure was a safety precaution for my well-being.

I know without a doubt that she agreed with me and fought for me because she's a woman. A male doctor just could not have understood my reasons; he could not have resonated with why it was so very important to me. I was not aware at the time that I had made such an unusual request, it felt very natural for me to do this.

The pathologist even called me to inquire if I was for real. He wanted the words from my own mouth as to why I wanted my womb back.

"My body is precious, a gift from God and I do not want it violated. I want to honor it for the wonderful service it performed for me," I explained.

"That little organ was the part of my body that allowed me to be a mother, which I consider to be my life's calling. Without it, I would not have been a mother and because of it, my children have been well-nurtured and protected while they were in such a delicate state of growth that they could not survive outside of my body."

He asked me what I would do with it.

"I am going to bury it in front of the statue of Mother Mary in my rose garden." I replied. The garden was in front of my apartment in the low-income project.

"You can not do that, there are laws preventing the burial of any part of a living being unless they are interred by a funeral director," he replied.

"People bury birds and small animals all the time," I said. "All living things eventually go back to Mother Earth as part of nature's way. My uterus is not that big and I want to return my womb back to Mother Earth where she came from in the first place."

"I am going to do it!" I insisted. "Either I get my womb back or I refuse the hysterectomy."

He then explained that he would have to use formaldehyde as part of the procedure and that "it could be dangerous to the land."

"It will be in a container," I countered.

"You cannot bury any container," he said.

I thought about it and could not imagine placing my womb in a container that would go back to Mother Earth naturally. It needed a proper shroud and proper burial. AHA! A shroud I could furnish.

"I am going to wrap it in an antique cotton handkerchief with lace," I said.

He finally agreed to allow it. He would rinse off as much of the formaldehyde as he could. He terminated the call with, "Lady, I sure hope you don't start a fad."

I chuckled. I was not trying to do anything but what I felt was true to my heart. Divine Inspiration?

Hey girls! Would you like to start a fad?

The operation was not for a month, so I had time to prepare for all that was to transpire. First I had to choose the place of reverence. I had a statue of Mother Mary with rose plants all around her. I went outside and dug a hole in front of her, big enough to bury my womb. I saved the dirt for after the internment and I placed a rock on top of the hole to keep animals out and to keep it from being filled back in. The surgery was scheduled for late fall so I knew the ground would be frozen and I would not be able to dig a hole after the operation. I wanted something biodegradable to place it in, so I found that cotton handkerchief of my mother's. I originally had come from my mother's womb and now she would still be nurturing me. She was in the nursing home and would not be able to attend the ceremony I had planned but her spirit would definitely be there.

I knew it would be a fitting shroud and the burial spot was perfect. What greater place could I have chosen than to be in front of the Divine Mother? She would watch over my womb and it would be enveloped with the love of Mother Earth.

During the preparations, I kept the secret to myself. But then I was told I would not be able to bring it home with me when I was discharged from the hospital. I would have to claim it after a week, so I let my best friend of fifty years in on my secret. Thank God for friends. Rose, bless her heart, did not laugh at me and agreed to do it. I knew I was asking a big favor. How many people do you know that would do you such an outrageous favor?

"I cannot believe I am going to the hospital to pick up your uterus," she said. "I wouldn't do this for anyone but you."

She was so leery of doing this that she asked her husband to do it but he refused. "I do a lot for you but this I cannot do," he said. I did not fully understand the enormity of what I was asking of her and did not realize that fact until many years later.

That is what I call a best friend.

It felt so normal and right for me to do this that I never considered it strange or out of the ordinary. Rose later told me how difficult it was for her to actually carry a part of my body. She felt strange, as though everyone was staring at her. She felt guilty, as though she was doing something wrong. Her thought was that if anyone knew, they might lock her up on a funny farm.

"I felt like I was doing something wrong, like I was stealing something that did not belong to me. I expected to be stopped at any moment and be exposed and arrested," she said.

She laughed as she said that going to the hospital and asking for and carrying around my womb was not anything she ever dreamed she would or could do. She had me laughing as she described her "trip." She went to the appointed place and told them who she was. They asked her my name and then gave her a small jar.

The person giving it to her said, "She must be a good friend of yours if you would do this for her."

Rose then asked if it could be put in a paper bag. They never asked her for identification. Here she felt like she was doing something illegal and the whole episode was treated like it was an everyday occurrence!

"It was all done so casually," Rose told me. "As I walked through the hospital to get to my car, it felt like I was in a story that you see on TV, it felt so surreal."

"I was shaking so much, I was surprised that no one noticed or, at the very least, asked me if I was okay. I could just imagine telling another person that I was carrying my best friend's womb. I bet no one else has ever done this."

I asked her if she wanted to see, but she declined. I hugged her so tightly for being such a good friend and for accomplishing this feat that I could not do myself.

After she had left, I seemed to enter a different time zone. I wanted so much to see this incredible organ but I was scared at the same time. The whole scene did not feel real to me. Was I actually doing this?

My hands trembled as I opened the bag. I saw a plastic container. I was amazed at how small the organ actually was. Considering the size of a baby, it brought me to the realization of how much it had needed to stretch and grow to accommodate the bodies of my babies. The insights of that understanding made me love and treasure it even that much more. This was my children's first home.

I had not mentioned to my children what I was planning to do. I was afraid that my children and friends would think I had "gone off my rocker." I quietly did all the preparations.

I knew I would receive my womb (the wounded chalice) two days before Thanksgiving, so I asked all my children to visit me at the same time for the Thanksgiving holiday.

They all agreed even if they were surprised at the request. Come Thanksgiving, my oldest son Dave, his wife and child; my daughter Sarah and my granddaughter, age 10; and my youngest son Max all gathered in my living room.

Because of the hysterectomy, I was not allowed to climb stairs so my bed had been brought down to the living room on the first floor. I was still living in public housing. I was poor again, with no assets to my name, but at this moment, I felt rich. I had my family with me and I had so many things to be grateful for. The listings of gratitude would have filled an entire sheet of paper and perhaps more.

I called my children a little away from the others. They gathered around me and I need to admit I was terrified. Do "normal" mothers do this? I did not know, but I told them what I had done.

My eldest son Dave has a way of playing on words, hoping to bring humor to any situation. When I mentioned that my womb had a hole in it, he quipped, "A womb (room) with a view!"

Of course it brought forth some nervous laughter but not from me. At this, my daughter Sarah gave him a look that said, "not now."

"Dave, be nice," she added.

I was physically shaking and quite serious as I proceeded. My daughter, being a female herself, understood the seriousness of this occasion and the solemnity of it. Her brothers did not understand but they could see how important it was to me so they honored it.

Including them in this ceremony was so important to me that I started to cry and addressed them saying: "I brought you all here today to honor the first home you ever knew, the part of me that nurtured you and protected you from harm. It cared for you when I could not physically touch you. It knew you before I knew you."

Then I addressed them individually:

"Dave, you are my first born. I was so overwhelmed with awe at your little body when you came into this world. I never knew such fulfillment and joy. I had not known how to take care of you but my body did. I was new to all the changes happening in my body, but, without any prior experience, my womb kept you safe, healthy and growing until your body was strong enough to come out into this world.

"Sarah, you are my second child. By now, I thought I knew what to expect of my body in pregnancy, but my body carried you completely different than your older brother. It knew you were female and needed to be carried round instead of like a football. My womb cared for you the way you needed to be cared for, what was special just for you. Birthing you was such a joy as my body had already been stretched and was more willing to give of its fruit much sooner.

"I would like to honor both of my miscarriages that occurred after my first two births. I know my body was exercising its wisdom.

"Max, you are my youngest child. You above the others need to be thankful to this organ. The doctors said you would never be normal, either mentally or physically. They wanted to abort you. Although in my humanness I did not want to care for a special needs child, in my heart, I could not destroy you. God had created you and who was I to question His Wisdom. It was with great reverence that my body cared for and protected you and allowed you to be born 'normal' in every way. This part of my body nourished you and loved you all the while I was worrying about your well-being."

My kids had tears in their eyes and were a little aghast at what I had done. I explained how I had prepared the place where the womb would be buried. I asked them to come outside with me for the burial. Respecting the first home they ever knew, they honored my request with dignity.

I was still shaking as the awareness of what I had done descended upon me. Until then, everything I did felt perfectly normal but now I realized the steps I had taken were not the norm. My children's reactions opened my eyes and heart at last to the real solemnity of the occasion. It was an unusual and unorthodox reason for this family gathering.

Dave, with his sense of humor, said a few funny things to relieve the seriousness and asked how, with the ground frozen, were we going to do this? After a few comments and chuckles about the womb with a view, we got down to business.

They were amazed to see how I had prepared. They were brought up Catholic but do not practice their religion, although I heard some voices following me when I said the Hail Mary and the Our Father.

"Mother Earth," I said, "receive the part of my body that I no longer need. From dirt you were conceived and back to dirt you shall return. Beloved womb, I thank you for your invaluable service to me and to my children."

I asked Dave to remove the rock.

"You lucked out, you avoided the meat grinder," Dave said to the minute package in the shroud, trying to lighten the tension.

I gave the handkerchief with its contents to Sarah. She placed the little packet in the hole. I noticed that she was shaking, too. It felt like we were suspended in time.

Max placed the dirt I had saved on top of the shroud and replaced the rock. He had tears in his eyes.

My uterus was at rest in front of our Lady and would give life to the roses that were planted there. It was very appropriate as the smell of roses is Mother's signature and the rose is my favorite flower, especially ones that have a scent.

I was so emotional and overwhelmed. I felt complete and was so grateful that my children had participated in the ceremony with no hesitation. It would not have been complete without them.

My mind shut down and would not allow me to remember what happened next. I do not remember what was said afterward as we rejoined their families in the house. I know my children and their families must have left afterwards but I have no conscious memory of it. I had dissociated again.

"Beloved children, I am so grateful to you for being you and for allowing me to be me."

15
CALL OF THE DIVINE FEMININE

A year later, I went to Mt. Shasta, California on a yearly retreat. I met a woman who brought forth the Spirit of the Divine Feminine, Mother Mary. I told her what had happened to me and how I handled it. She said that I was to write a book about my experience as that would lead women to value their femininity and their awesome role of bringing *LOVE* into the world. She told me also to get a Silver Chalice that was to be the picture on the cover of my book and that the title of the book was to be *The Wounded Chalice*.

At the time I winced because I do not care for silver, as it tarnishes and requires a lot of care to keep it clean. I was also overwhelmed with the possibility of writing a book. I do not know how to write and I was quite shy and reticent about being in the public eye.

I felt a little uneasy about owning a Chalice, I did not feel worthy, and so I did some research to help me accept what was being asked of me. This is what I found.

The Chalice is the most important of all the vessels in church use. The Chalice in a particular way was identified with the priesthood. The Chalice occupies the first place among sacred vessels. The material cup is often used as if it was synonymous with the Precious Blood itself. "The Chalice of Benediction, which we bless," writes St. Paul, "is it not the Communion of the Blood of Christ?" (1 Corinthians 10:16)

I looked up the meaning of the word Chalice from Wikipedia: "A Chalice (from Latin 'calix', cup) is a goblet intended to hold drink. In general religious terms, it is a goblet intended for drinking some beverage during a ceremony."

"The Holy Grail is sometimes thought to have been a Chalice. The Chalice symbolizes the central place of communion in worship for the Christian Church (*Disciples of Christ*)."

"As the Sacramental Cup, it signifies Faith." (*New Catholic Dictionary*)

In *Development of Christian Legends*, the Holy Chalice has often been identified with the Holy Grail, which is said to be the cup used to catch Jesus' dripping blood when he was on the cross or the chalice that Joseph of Arimethea used to collect Christ's blood upon his removal from the cross.

Herbert Thurston in the Catholic Encyclopedia of 1908 refers to the only record of a Chalice from the Last Supper as a two handled *SILVER* Chalice.

Percival, from a source book by Count Philip of Flanders, must prove himself worthy to be in The Grail's presence. In the early tales, his immaturity prevents him from fulfilling his destiny when he first encounters the Grail; he must grow spiritually and mentally before he can locate it again. In later tellings, the Grail is a symbol of God's Grace, available to all but only fully realized by those who prepare themselves spiritually.

Association of the Grail with the Sacrament of the Eucharist gives spiritual nourishment to the faithful.

"This cup which is poured out for you is the new covenant in my blood." (Luke 22:20)

All that happened in 1993 and I kept the words of the Mt. Shasta woman close to my heart. I could not financially afford to buy a Chalice so I looked for alternatives.

Diamonds are so beautiful and I like to look at them and admire them, but I believe that too high a price has been put on them. They are simply a rock that Mother Nature has made, along with thousands of other rocks that are also beautiful.

I admire all that Mother Nature creates, yet I resist saying that one is above the rest. I look at rocks as individual creations. They are a reminder to me of how individual we humans are. We were all created by God and, as such, are equally valuable in His eyes.

For Christmas in 1988, Sam had given me diamond earrings even though he knew that I did not like diamonds. I had showed Sam some jewelry I liked but did not feel I could spend the money on. Instead of pleasing me with what I wanted, he gave me what made him feel great. He had showed them to everyone he knew just to brag and was very surprised when I had enough courage to refuse them.

We had dated for seven years and when we planned to marry, I specifically told him I did not want a diamond. In order to get what he wanted, he waited until Christmas Eve, in front of his entire family, and proposed with a diamond ring. Since I loved him and did not want to embarrass him, I accepted it. Looking back now, it was the beginning of giving away the person I was in order to become who he wanted me to be. He was manipulating me and I was allowing it. It was a constant reminder of how little he had actually considered my wishes.

Looking him in the eyes when I said I would return the earrings, I knew he knew in his heart that the gift was going to be offensive to me but he wanted to be a big shot anyway. I think that was the beginning of my reclaiming my self-worth back, my own voice. I was finally being true to myself.

I did not accept the diamond earrings and took them back to the jeweler. They would not return our money and I was forced to choose something else. Of course there was only diamond jewelry to choose from, as it was a diamond jeweler's store. It was either take something with diamonds or lose the money he had paid for them. I refused to get anything with diamonds and insisted that he get a ring for himself.

I still cannot recall how it happened but I ended up with five different rings, all with diamonds. I hardly wore them and when I did it was only to please him. I only wish I had had the courage to walk right out of the store with nothing, leaving the earrings right there. I guess Spirit had something else in mind. I am telling this part of my story so you may realize how Spirit works even when we are not aware.

After our divorce, I had an inspiration to pawn the rings for money. Perhaps pawn is not the best word but I went to a business that bought and sold used jewelry. I had never been to this type of store before and chose this one from the phone book.

While I was there, I asked if they had a silver chalice. I was told no at first but then someone remembered a box out back and retrieved it. Inside this old black box was a Chalice in two pieces. To me it looked like gold and I was just going to refuse it when something guided me to look at it further.

My heart leapt, this was no ordinary Chalice. The base had six offshoot teardrops with figures of Biblical symbols. The first was of the Annunciation with Archangel Gabriel asking Mary to be the mother of Jesus. The second was the Birth of Jesus with Mary, Joseph and the three wise men. The third was The Presentation of Jesus in the Temple with Mary, Joseph, Simeon and Anna. The fourth was the Last Supper, Jesus with his twelve Apostles. The fifth was the cross in a circle with rays around it within the original circle signifying the Crucifixion. The sixth was the Resurrection, Christ rising into the clouds as His apostles watched.

There was engraving underneath the base in a foreign language. Someone told me the Chalice was designed and created for the ordination of a priest. The priest's name may have been part of the inscription. The year inscribed was 1913. Someday I hope to have the inscription translated.

I did not know whether I wanted this to be my Chalice or not. Sometimes when Spirit asks you to do something, there are mixed emotions about carrying it out. There were some dark spots on the Chalice that looked like they were tarnished. It was agreed that I take the chalice to a silversmith and ask him to verify the metal. I paid for it with three of my diamond rings and they agreed that if it could not be fixed, they would take it back and give me credit toward something else.

I only know that I was trying to clear my life of any articles that held a negative emotion for me. Even today, I am in awe of how Spirit uses all events in our life as guidance toward our destiny.

Finding someone who worked with silver proved difficult. Silver jewelry and silver pieces are in every jewelry shop, but to find someone willing to work on silver is very difficult. The silversmith I was finally led to had created a silver polish that is famous for its use by museums. I did not know if he could help me, but I went to see him anyway.

When he looked at the Chalice, he said that it was silver gilded with gold. It fascinated him. Gilded gold is rare and he happened to have some in his shop. He agreed to try to fix it as long as I would not hold him liable if something went wrong.

Gilding is a specialized process. More than 4,000 years ago, ancient civilizations of Egypt and China discovered that gold could be hammered between layers of animal skins. It was sometimes beaten with a rounded stone. This produced thin leaves (1/250,000 of an inch thick) that were translucent if held up to the light.

Gilding was ferociously difficult to work with, thinner than tissue paper, floating away at the slightest breath. It was then laid onto a substrate made of metal, wood, lacquer, plastic, etc. to give the item the appearance of being made of solid gold.

The gilding technique, sometimes called gold leaf gilding that was used in the past is the same gilding technique that is used today. Genuine gold leaf will not tarnish. Leaf that tarnishes is composition leaf, silver leaf, variegated leaf or copper leaf. Most gold leaf is of at least 22 carat purity, which is very soft.

The silversmith had the Chalice in his shop for a month. When he called to tell me it was ready he said it was the most difficult thing he had ever done. "Had I realized at the time how difficult it would be, I would never have agreed to try to fix it!" he said.

If we can release control we can then see so many synchronicities happening. I have a daily mantra, some days I say it more than once: "I release control and allow trust to be the center of my life. I express my needs and trust that they will be met."

As I look back on how many unusual things have happened to me and how so many people have shown up in my life just when I needed further guidance, I feel blessed.

I was thrilled with the Chalice's appearance and felt like I had completed part of the mission I was given. Today it sits on my altar as a symbol of my trust and willingness to listen to my own Divinely inspired guidance. When the Divine Feminine told me to write the story she also told me:

"A Chalice has been placed in your body where your womb used to be. Where once it held one soul at a time, it now holds the world."

I could not help but be aware of the symbolism of the Chalice and the womb. The Wounded Chalice is my womb that had been punctured by the doctor, thus creating the reality of a hysterectomy which then resulted in my request for the Chalice (womb) to be given back to me that I may honor the Gift of Life.

My womb had been punctured much like the heart of Jesus when He was crucified. We celebrate the Eucharist with a Chalice that contains the Blood of Christ. Both the womb and the Chalice offer life to us as earthly humans.

I had tried to write this book three times before, but each time something came up and I did not complete it. I am finally writing it with the guidance and urging of The Divine Mother.

Fellow brothers and sisters, I am writing this to let you know that you do have authority over your body. Each and every part of you is invaluable. One part of your body is not any more important than the other; however, my womb held those most dear to me, so it was the most important organ in order for me to fulfill my mission. I do not know why I chose this experience but Spirit is using me to share it with you.

Have you ever felt as natural as I did about a decision you have made? I know that it was the Holy Spirit who enveloped me with this idea and it was I who carried it to fruition with the love and encouragement of the Divine Feminine. Life experiences are meant to be just that, experiences. They are neither good nor bad just opportunities that we bring to ourselves so that we may more fully explore our humanness. I wish to thank all the players who participated in this drama that I have been inspired to share with you.

EPILOGUE

When my womb was examined after the hysterectomy, it was found to have no hole in it. A miracle? Part of me was not surprised by this. I know I was meant to pay homage to the Divine Feminine with the burial ceremony of my womb. I truly believe that all of this transpired that I might write this book and share it with you. It is amazing to me how we can know something at the soul level but fear of being ridiculed prevents us from expressing it verbally. I believe in miracles; however I am always pleasantly surprised when they show up. Was I being used to make others more aware of the love their bodies give to them? How else could all of these synchronicities be made manifest to prove that once you surrender your will to the Lord, He uses you to show others how much Love He has for them? How much we are taken care of, even when we are not consciously aware of His Divine Will! When you truly love yourself then you can truly love another. Listen to that small voice in your heart.

"Is it trying to tell you something?"

"Life is a drama on this stage called earth."

"What part of the drama are you choosing to play?"

My story is about a woman's self-worth. The emotions are the same for all of us regardless of "story." Lessons from life give us an awareness of choice and a rainbow after the storm. There *IS* a light at the end of the tunnel and it is not a train, it is the knowledge of the Divinity of everyone.

Earth is a school and we are fortunate enough to have many students accompany us along our way, making sure we experience and learn the lessons we chose to learn before we were born. Happiness is a choice and we choose that joy through the love of self and others. We gain confidence in our own truth by voicing what we believe.

My human journey was the crucible that prepared me to fulfill my promise to Mother. The events that shaped my life and the preconditioning that dictated my choices were a blessing in disguise. Although they did not feel like blessings, hindsight has shown me that I would not be who I am today or even where I am today without those events.

Today I live on a lake in a small town where it is blissfully quiet. I have many birds to watch and the water which has a life of its own. I need only my small house and not a mansion to live in. My children are grown with children of their own and I have the ability to see the rainbow after the storm. Without that storm, I would not have the rainbow or any of the deep peace that envelops me.

I am being guided to write another book which will pick up where this one ends and chronicles my spiritual journey into the discovery of myself. Be not afraid of the storm; always look for the rainbow because it will appear. The light at the end of the tunnel was for me a light from Beloved Jesus and Mary. They brought me from the depths of despair and frustration into recognizing that God is in everyone. Everyone has a piece of God within and the only requirement to know that is to allow yourself to see the piece that is within you. Love yourself and you will love others. Forgive yourself and you will forgive others. You cannot help it. That is called Unconditional Love. Mother's love is a pure example of this.

THE QUESTION OF LOVE IS ONE THAT CANNOT BE EVADED.

WHETHER OR NOT YOU CLAIM TO BE INTERESTED IN IT, FROM THE MOMENT YOU ARE ALIVE YOU ARE BOUND TO BE CONCERNED WITH LOVE, BECAUSE LOVE IS NOT JUST SOMETHING THAT HAPPENS TO YOU:

IT IS A CERTAIN SPECIAL WAY OF BEING ALIVE. LOVE IS, IN FACT, AN INTENSIFICATION OF LIFE. COMPLETENESS, FULLNESS, AND A WHOLENESS OF LIFE. - THOMAS MERTON

SURPRISE GIFT WAITING FOR YOU

I REALLY CARE ABOUT YOUR OPINION.

MY WISH IS TO TOUCH MANY PEOPLE LIKE YOU.

CAN YOU HELP ME?

If you choose to fill out a short survey on the website listed below, there is a surprise gift waiting for you.

http://www.TheWoundedChalice.com

Thank you sincerely,

Love and Light,

Mary Grace

A READER'S GUIDE

A reader's guide and reflections are available in addition to discussion questions for small groups on the website:

http://www.TheWoundedChalice.com

mailto:thewoundedchalice@gmail.com

ABOUT THE AUTHOR

Mary Grace, B.S, R.M.T. is a student of life who has survived and conquered fears and losses which have given her a unique view of the world. Beginning with a teenage marriage and motherhood, she realized that only by conquering her fears could she be an example for her children to follow. These fears felt huge to her, as all fears do, even if they seemed unfounded to the onlooker.

Confrontation was not her strong suit unless it was for the sake of one of her young ones. She became a tigress when one of her children was threatened or harmed in any way. It took a lot of courage to let her children pursue their own paths especially when it was not what she wanted in her heart for them.

To be a mother was her only dream and she expected that to be her whole life. She was not anticipating a career; she only wanted to obtain a college degree because she loved to learn new things. Well, life had something totally different in mind. Finally she earned a Bachelor's Degree at age 52, but the most important things she learned came from the school of hard knocks. All these knocks were opportunities for a different experience enabling her to come away with a degree in Living.

Mary Grace learned to stand up and confront life with all of its challenges which strengthened her resolve to be courageous as well as loving and forgiving. Finding the courage to "hear" her inner voice has led her to make decisions that have been life changing. When the Divine Feminine told her to write this book, she was surprised as well as pleased with the assignment.

Although she always won the spelling bees in school and still can readily spot a misspelled word, she never thought of actually writing a book. In order to fulfill Mother's wish, she attended a writing class taught by the editor of a column in the daily newspaper. The final project in this class was to read a rough draft of what she had written. She found that everyone in the class seemed to have been touched by different passages; the women had tears in their eyes and the men were also visibly affected. They had differing opinions on what type of magazine would most likely print the article about reclaiming her womb after a hysterectomy. Some suggestions were: health magazines, women's magazines, spiritual magazines, mother magazines, self – help magazines, etc. This class enabled her to gain insights into writing this book.

Over the last 15 years, Mary Grace attempted to complete *The Wounded Chalice*. After all, Mother had already given her the title of the book and guided her to locate the "right" chalice. Evidently the timing was not yet right. For the last two years she has worked to fulfill what she had been asked to accomplish.

She experienced the joys and challenges of motherhood, two failed marriages, an IRS lien and loss of all material goods while gaining spiritual strength and depth. She has come full circle. She has been honed and primed to share this message with you. Mary Grace is a Reiki Master, Speaker, Eucharistic Minister, Reader for the Blind, Hospice Volunteer, Toastmaster, and has been a guest on the local TV Show, *Down Under*.

Her home in Massachusetts is on the water; it is peaceful, comforting and interesting with all the birds that visit the feeders. The water has a life of its own; it constantly changes even in winter. It is a perfect example of her life with its myriad of changes. She now lives in peace and harmony and wishes to express the truth that she garnered from every challenge.

Mary Grace has traveled to many spiritual sites looking for her truth, looking for herself, looking for answers. She is like a bud that is unfolding and her next book will detail her spiritual journey. There was something pulling and tugging at her, prodding her to find out who she really was. Who was she after the children grew up and started their own lives?

To request Mary Grace to speak at your gatherings or to contact her, you may email her at:

mailto:thewoundedchalice@gmail.com.

You are invited to visit Mary Grace's web site at:
http://www.thewoundedchalice.com

Printed in the United States
201901BV00002B/625-684/P